THE CEO'S BOSS

WILLIAM M. KLEPPER

THE CEO'S BOSS

TOUGH
LOVE
IN THE
BOARDROOM

Columbia Business School
Publishing

Columbia University Press
Publishers Since 1893
New York   Chichester, West Sussex
Copyright © 2010 Columbia University Press
All rights reserved
Library of Congress Cataloging-in-Publication Data

Klepper, William M.
The CEO's boss : tough love in the boardroom / William Klepper.
    p.   cm.
Includes bibliographical references and index.
ISBN 978-0-231-14988-4 (alk. paper) — ISBN 978-0-231-52063-8 (ebook)
1. Chief executive officers.   2. Corporate governance.   3. Decision making.
4. Leadership.   I. Title.

HD38.2.K58 2010
658.4'22—dc22

2010006617

Columbia University Press books are printed on permanent and durable acid-free
paper.
This book is printed on paper with recycled content.
Printed in the United States of America
c 10 9 8 7 6 5 4 3
References to Internet Web sites (URLs) were accurate at the time of writing. Neither
the author nor Columbia University Press is responsible for URLs that may have
expired or changed since the manuscript was prepared.

CONTENTS

ACKNOWLEDGMENTS

I could not have written *The CEO's Boss: Tough Love in the Boardroom* without the encouragement and support of a number of Columbia Business School colleagues. Rita McGrath, the most prolific writer among our Executive Education faculty team (her latest offering being *Discovery-Driven Growth: A Breakthrough Process to Reduce Risk and Seize Opportunity,* 2009) was my central catalyst. We were delayed by weather on one of our return flights from Buffalo, NY, after working with M&T Bank. During that three-hour layover at the airport we wrote the initial outline for the book. David Beim, whose case study of Take Two Interactive is the cornerstone of chapter 5, was my entrée into working with the Outstanding Directors Exchange (ODX). David, after a 25-year career in investment banking, is now Professor of Professional Practice at Columbia Business School. His recent writing on the root cause of our financial crisis is indicative of his insight, such as his March 2009 article in *Forbes,* "It's All About Debt: Who Caused the Global Economic Collapse? We All Did." Bill Duggan, the author of three recent books on strategic intuition as the key to innovation—*Napoleon's Glance: The Secret of Strategy* (2002); *The Art of What Works: How Success Really Happens* (2003); and *Strategic Intuition: The Creative Spark in Human Achievement* (2007)—was my soul mate in my work with Columbia Business School Publishing (CBSP). He encouraged me in my journey and alerted me to the talents of Myles Thompson, publisher, and Marina Petrova, assistant editor. In addition, I want to give a special thanks to Bridget Flannery-McCoy, the editorial assistant who was assigned to do the final developmental and fine editing of the book—she understood "tough love" and how it could make this author's writing even better. Finally, my grateful recognition of the help of Troy Eggers, Associate Dean of Executive Education, who brokered my work to CBSP and told them of the Executive Education faculty's proven record of translating the school's thought leadership into practice—as in the works of Eric Abrahamsen, David Beim, Joel Brockner, Noel Capon, Mike Fenlon, Don Hambrick, Rita McGrath, Willie Pietersen, and Mike Tushman, which are referenced in the book.

I have had the privilege to serve over the last 3 years as the faculty director of the ODX/Columbia Business School partnership. During that time I have worked with a team of professionals who have supported my case work and presentations to directors at their ODX meetings in New York, Chicago, and San Francisco. Special thanks goes to Maureen Neary, executive director of ODX; Janet O'Neil, program director of ODX; Heather Wolf, director of the Outstanding Directors Program and the annual classes of Outstanding Director winners; and Gavin Daley, executive editor and managing director at Money-Media, a *Financial Times* company and producer of ODX.

Finally, I want to acknowledge Susan Klepper, my fellow faculty member at Columbia University, who models tough love in our family boardroom. Bill, Caroline, and Michael, our children, can attest to her skill and the effects that this love has had on their leadership in business and in life. This book is dedicated to them and their ongoing success.

THE CEO'S BOSS

1

The Social Contract

The heart of the idea of the social contract may be stated simply: Each of us places his person and authority under the supreme direction of the general will, and the group receives each individual as an indivisible part of the whole. . . .

JEAN-JACQUES ROUSSEAU, *THE SOCIAL CONTRACT*

Directors and CEO's alike are entrusted with remarkable responsibilities. The key to the successful leadership of a company is a strong partnership between these two parties. With the collapse of the housing market and the bankruptcy of such giants as Lehman Brothers and General Motors, the importance of this relationship has come sharply into focus, and it has become increasingly clear that CEO's cannot be held solely accountable for failures such as these. When the news of Lehman's demise broke, for instance, the question raised by the *Wall Street Journal* was, "Where was Lehman's board?" It noted, "As the world nervously awaits the effects of the unprecedented Lehman Brothers liquidation, one can't help but wonder how and why this board let its longtime chairman and patron, Richard Fuld Jr., cling to both hope and power."[1] It is time to reexamine the role of the board and to explore how board members can best achieve their role as "the CEO's boss."

A Productive Partnership: Tyco

If an unsuccessful relationship between the board and the CEO can lead to disaster, then a productive one can help restore or avert it. A recent success story is the rescue of Tyco International through the partnership of Jack Krol, lead director, and his CEO/chairman, Edward D. Breen. Breen, previously the president and COO of Motorola, was appointed the new chairman and CEO of Tyco in 2002 and came to the company in the midst of a devastating failure in leadership. The former chairman and CEO Dennis Kozlowski and former CFO Mark H. Swartz had been accused of stealing $600 million from the company, and in 2005, after a retrial, both men were sentenced to 8 to 25 years in prison.

Breen believed that drastic change was needed to save the company, and he saw it as his responsibility to be hard on the problems facing Tyco. Bringing a world-class leadership team with him, he immediately acted to stabilize the company and restore shareholder confidence. To this end, he committed to replacing the board of directors and the leadership team under Kozlowski with a team of independent directors. In August 2002, with the priority of improving the company's corporate governance, Breen announced the appointment of Jack Krol as lead director.[2] Like Breen, Krol believed that big changes and tough decisions were necessary to get the company back on track. The stage was set for a partnership based on strong but shared beliefs.

By the end of 2005, Tyco's revenue had reached nearly $40 billion under this leadership team. However, despite the company's renewed success, on January 13, 2006, Tyco and its board of directors announced its intent to separate Tyco into three distinct, publicly traded companies. According to Breen:

> In the past several years, Tyco has come a long way. Our balance sheet and cash flows are strong and many legacy financial and legal issues have been resolved. We are fortunate to have a great mix of businesses with market-leading positions. After a thorough review of strategic options with our Board of Directors, we have determined that separating into three independent companies is the best approach to enable these businesses to achieve their full potential.[3]

This decision further emphasized the difference between the dysfunctional leaders that had left and the pro-active team that had taken their place. Following the separation, Breen remained at the head of Tyco International.

In October 2007, at a meeting of the Outstanding Directors Exchange (ODX) in Chicago, I attended a table discussion with Jack Krol in which he and Ed Breen discussed the recent changes that had taken place within the company. Although their presentation on the separation was interesting, what was most compelling to the audience was the story that Krol and Breen told about their partnership as lead director and CEO/chairman. The men talked about how they maintained a successful relationship by being clear with each other on their strategy, priorities, and the gaps they had to close. Coming into the job, both knew that the business was in a turnaround stage in its life cycle and that they had to challenge the status quo and make informed decisions to save Tyco.

Adding force to their determination was their collective commitment to their Ethical Conduct and Board Governance Principles, a document that acted as a Social Contract to promote and ensure integrity, compliance, and accountability. Breen and Krol, in their presentation at ODX, emphasized how these three principles were the foundation for their partnership. Without these behavioral standards, they could not have clearly defined the change they envisioned for Tyco. Over their 5 years together, these three principles were expanded to today's Tyco Vision and Values.

TYCO VISION AND VALUES

Tyco International's Board of Directors is responsible for directing, and providing oversight of, the management of Tyco's business in the best interests of the shareholders and consistent with good corporate citizenship. In carrying out its responsibilities, the board selects and monitors top management, provides oversight for financial reporting and legal compliance, determines Tyco's governance principles and implements its governance policies. The board, together with management, is responsible for establishing the firm's operating values and code of conduct and for setting strategic direction and priorities.

While Tyco's strategy and leadership evolve in response to its changing market conditions, the company's vision and values are enduring. So too are five governance principles, and along with the company's vision and values, they constitute the foundation upon which the company's governance policies are built.

Tyco believes that good governance requires not only an effective set of specific practices but also a culture of responsibility throughout the firm, and governance at Tyco is intended to optimize both. Tyco also believes that good governance ultimately depends on the quality of its leadership, and it is committed to recruiting and retaining directors and officers of proven leadership and personal integrity.

TYCO VISION: WHY WE EXIST AND
THE ESSENCE OF OUR BUSINESS

To be our customers' first choice in every market we serve by exceeding commitments, providing new technology solutions, leveraging our diverse brands, driving operational excellence, and committing to the highest standards of business practices—all of which will lead to Tyco's long-term growth, value, and success.

TYCO VALUES: HOW WE CONDUCT OURSELVES

Integrity: We demand of each other and ourselves the highest standards of individual and corporate integrity with our customers, suppliers, vendors, agents and stakeholders. We vigorously protect company assets and comply with all company policies and laws.

Excellence: We continually challenge each other to improve our products, our processes and ourselves. We strive always to understand our customers' and suppliers' businesses and help them achieve their goals. We are dedicated to diversity, fair treatment, mutual respect and trust of our employees and customers.

Teamwork: We foster an environment that encourages innovation, creativity and results through teamwork and mutual respect. We practice leadership that teaches, inspires and promotes full participation and career development. We encourage open and effective communication and interaction.

Accountability: We will meet the commitments we make and take personal responsibility for all actions and results. We will create an operating discipline of continuous improvement that will be integrated into our culture."[4]

Jack Krol left the Tyco board in March 2008, but his reputation as an "outstanding director" was acknowledged at ODX in 2007. Quoting from the *Agenda* article that profiled Krol's accomplishment: "When Breen signed on, he believed that Tyco's core manufacturing businesses were solid, but he wasn't sure how far across the organization the corruption reached. Nor was he exactly sure how to avoid bankruptcy. He needed a partner, and fast. . . . Krol's reputation and total commitment to the task were major factors in both saving the company and restoring its respectability."[5]

Prescription: The Social Contract

A Social Contract, if developed correctly, can provide a prescription for strengthening and maintaining the partnership between the board and its CEO. I am defining a Social Contract as a clear set of behavioral statements willingly subscribed to by the board and CEO that details the mutual expectations of their partnership. In layman's terms, the Social Contract puts forth "the rules of the road." The roots of the Social Contract are in the postconventional moral reasoning that is at the core of a democratic government. (See Kohlberg's Moral Development Theory, Stage 5, which is Social Contract driven.[6]) As an alumnus of Saint Louis University, I consider my education Jesuit in nature, with a core emphasis on philosophy and all its applications. Thus, although my real academic focus was management, I have maintained an interest in the philosophy behind it. The Social Contract is particularly interesting to me, as it is fundamentally a philosophical document that results from a philosophical discussion. It is a contract between a board and its CEO that is developed through a conversation about what's important to ensure their commitment to the welfare of the business. *Each of us places his person and authority under the supreme direction of the general will*—in this case, the board/CEO partnership.

From my experience as a board chairman, I have found that the best way to start a discussion of a board/CEO Social Contract is to come up with five behavioral standards to present to the CEO. Five is a deliberate choice— I'm a believer in Miller's law, the work of cognitive psychologist George A. Miller of Princeton University's Department of Psychology, who measured human short-term memory capacity and found a 7 ± 2 limit.[7] I prefer keeping the number at the lower end of the range so that the standards can be readily remembered. The five I use are

- *Commitment to values:* a leadership credo that answers the question, "What do we stand for as an organization?"
- *Commitment to the stakeholders:* customers, employees, shareholders, and community.
- *Commitment to risk assessment:* a willingness to manage the company's risk profile.
- *Commitment to transparency:* complete honesty in financial and nonfinancial matters.
- *Commitment to coaching:* supporting the CEO and board's continuous improvement.

These five standards can help the board consider the critical aspects of the company and discuss its general leadership expectations.

Commitment to Values

I've worked with a number of boards to develop a leadership credo by articulating an answer to the question, "What do we stand for as an organization?" It may sound simple, but it goes to the core of the way things are done around the organization—its culture. The culture of the company dictates the general will and behavior of the CEO and the board.

Johnson & Johnson has one of the most noteworthy credo statements of any company. As the company states on its Web site:

> The values that guide our decision making are spelled out in Our Credo. . . . Robert Wood Johnson, former chairman from 1932 to 1963 and a member of the Company's founding family, crafted Our Credo himself in 1943, just before Johnson & Johnson became a publicly traded company. This was long before anyone ever heard the term "corporate social responsibility." Our Credo is more than just a moral compass. We believe it's a recipe for business success. The fact that Johnson & Johnson is one of only a handful of companies that have flourished through more than a century of change is proof of that.[8]

OUR CREDO

We believe our first responsibility is to the doctors, nurses and patients, to mothers and fathers and all others who use our products and services. In meeting their needs, everything we do must be of high quality. We must constantly strive to reduce our costs in order to maintain reasonable prices. Customers' orders must be serviced promptly and accurately. Our suppliers and distributors must have an opportunity to make a fair profit.

We are responsible to our employees, the men and women who work with us throughout the world. Everyone must be considered as an individual. We must respect their dignity and recognize their merit. They must have a sense of security in their jobs. Compensation must be fair and adequate, and working conditions clean, orderly and safe.

We must be mindful of ways to help our employees fulfill their family responsibilities. Employees must feel free to make suggestions and complaints. There must be equal opportunity for employment, development and advancement for those qualified. We must provide competent management, and their actions must be just and ethical.

We are responsible to the communities in which we live and work and to the world community as well. We must be good citizens— support good works and charities and bear our fair share of taxes. We must encourage civic improvements and better health and education. We must maintain in good order the property we are privileged to use, protecting the environment and natural resources.

Our final responsibility is to our stockholders. Business must make a sound profit. We must experiment with new ideas. Research must be carried on, innovative programs developed and mistakes paid for. New equipment must be purchased, new facilities provided and new products launched. Reserves must be created to provide for adverse times. When we operate according to these principles, the stockholders should realize a fair return.[9]

A joint commitment to a common set of instrumental values between the board and the CEO is central to a healthy partnership. Without a collective agreement as to the company's values, the leadership team will not have a complete set of tools to navigate through good and bad times.

In 1982, Johnson & Johnson proved just how committed it was to its Credo, and how the Credo helped shape strategic decisions, with its response to the Tylenol crisis. On September 29th of that year, a 12-year-old from Chicago died after taking a capsule of Extra Strength Tylenol. Another Chicagoan died shortly thereafter, as did his brother and sister-in-law after taking pills from the same bottle. There were two more deaths in the area before investigators discovered the Tylenol link. They believed that someone had stolen bottles of Tylenol off the shelves of various supermarkets, poisoned them with solid cyanide, and then replaced the bottles. This suspicion was confirmed when three doctored bottles were found in supermarkets.

I have worked with a number of "Big Pharma" companies and have referenced Johnson & Johnson's response to this incident as a clear example of a company that stuck to its credo in a crisis. The company warned hospitals and distributors, issued a nationwide recall of Tylenol products, and offered to exchange all capsules already purchased by the public with solid tablets. This recall of Tylenol products had a retail value of more than $100 million.

These decisions were strategic and could only have been guided by a clear set of principles that served as both a moral compass and a recipe for business success in a time of crisis. As a result, Tylenol was able to navigate through this difficult time with the Tylenol brand intact. The market share of Tylenol, which collapsed from 35% to 8%, rebounded in less than a year, and the brand regained its former popularity after coming back on the market in a triple-sealed package.

Commitment to the Stakeholders

One of my custom clients at Executive Education refers to his list of stakeholders as the "four legs of the stool" of the business. If any one of the legs is weak, the entire organization is out of balance. If you look back at the Johnson & Johnson Credo, you'll see that these four stakeholders constitute the focus of the company's values, and all four were considered in its reaction to the Tylenol crisis.

M&T Bank is another example of a company with a clear commitment to its stakeholders. Its Vision Statement reads, "M&T strives to be the best company our employees ever work for, the best bank our customers ever do business with and the best investment our shareholders ever make."[10] It then speaks about its role in the community: "M&T Bank has a long tradition of being involved in the cities, towns and neighborhoods in which we operate. As a community bank, we understand that the well-being of our company is connected to the well-being of the communities we serve."[11] This clear statement of commitments has helped M&T Bank's longtime CEO and chairman, Bob Wilmers, and his board turn the business into one of the twenty largest bank holding companies in the United States. A recent article in *Fortune* magazine captured the essence of M&T's Credo in its lead headline, "Banking the Buffalo way: At a time of crisis in the financial system, the big boys could learn a lot from the success of a thriving regional player, M&T Bank."[12]

In Columbia Executive Education's M&T Bank Executive Leadership, which I directed from 2006 through 2008, we focused on strategic management, leadership, and growth. I saw a calm resolve from the company at the onset of the banking crisis in 2008, and this attitude was based on the executives' shared commitment to employees, customers, shareholders, and the communities they serve. Without this credo, I doubt M&T could have weathered the turbulence of its industry.

Commitment to Risk Assessment

The recent financial crisis has highlighted the importance of risk management, and it is incumbent on boards to see that the CEO makes a commitment to manage the firm's strategic risk profile. A failure in risk management was one of the major factors in the Lehman collapse, and when the company went under, the press asked, "How much was Lehman's board monitoring the company's risk as it began accumulating its portfolio of real-estate assets and securities? In 2006 and 2007, the board's risk committee met twice each year, according to SEC filings."[13]

Michael Raynor's research has shown that a compelling vision, bold leadership, and decisive action, even though they are the prerequisites of success, are almost always present in failure as well. In his book *Innovator's Solution*, written with Clayton Christensen, he talked about maximizing the results of the business, but in his book *The Strategy Paradox: Why Committing to Success Leads Corporations to Failure . . . and What to Do About It*, he confronts the realities of managing risk.[14] His research calls on boards and CEO's to design their organizations so that managers at every level of the hierarchy understand the time horizon and degree of strategic uncertainty they deal with in order to make the right strategic choices. He introduces the phrase "Requisite Uncertainty" to describe this organizational design principle.

In 2007, right after the release of *The Strategy Paradox*, I was a participant on a podcast panel with Michael Raynor in which we discussed the book's content and implications. At the time, it was more in vogue to discuss maximizing results than to consider risk management. Now, only a few years later, it's clear that Raynor was onto something crucial. In today's economic crisis, boards and CEO's need to make a commitment to manage their risk if they are to survive.

Commitment to Transparency

In an ideal world, it would be a given, rather than a behavioral expectation, that a company's CEO is honest. In reality, it's important for the board/CEO Social Contract to make it clear that complete honesty is essential. This can help avoid gray areas by necessitating, for instance, full rather than partial disclosure. When CEO's withhold information from the board because they know it will be read as bad news, this is not dishonesty, but it isn't complete honesty either. When a Social Contract is developed correctly, the board and CEO establish the mutual expectation of full disclosure, which will help them solve their problems together. The underlying ethic is that this partnership is "hard on problems, not on people," and that the bearer of bad news should not be held immediately responsible. Although the ideal of "complete honesty" is hard to achieve in practice, the Social Contract does hold the board/CEO partnership to a commitment to transparency as the code of behavior. Transparency, when used in a Social Contract, implies openness, communication, and accountability.

The collapse of Lehman Brothers illustrates how a failure in transparent communication between the board and the CEO can lead to disaster. Most objective observers have concluded that Fuld did not fully disclose Lehman's financial matters, nor was there an honest assessment of nonfinancial matters, such as Fuld's leadership, by the board. Bad news was withheld until too late. The price that Lehman Brothers paid for these errors of omission or co-mission will be the work of the FBI investigation and lawsuits brought by its shareholders.

Commitment to Coaching

It has become common practice for boards to support the continuous improvement of their CEO's performance and to provide a professional coach to assist in the CEO's professional development. CEO's should be allowed to choose, with the agreement of the board, the coach that they feel can best provide helpful resources. I've served as a coach for a number of CEO's, and I've learned that the strength of the relationship between the coach and the CEO translates into a comparable strength in the partnership between the board and CEO.

In many instances, my first conversation with a new CEO client begins with a query of how things are going with the board. Inevitably, the CEO's will bring up the concerns of the board and one or more areas of the CEO's performance that are bothering them. I usually structure the rest of my coaching sessions around determining the root cause of these performance gaps and exploring the implications for the CEO's agenda, practices, and style. These are the various aspects of the CEO's behavior, and I explain them more fully in chapter 3. In the end, the goal is to align the CEO's performance with the needs of the business, and to determine what is required to close any remaining performance gaps.

However, continuous development goes beyond coaching for the CEO. The board has a comparable need to improve its skills and abilities in corporate governance. During the last three years, I have worked with ODX in its nationwide educational meetings. These directors-only conferences cover the most challenging boardroom issues. In addition, members are provided ongoing research and information through ODX publications like *Agenda*. Columbia Executive Education is another organization that offers support to board members by coaching directors to higher levels of performance in their corporate governance role.

The Social Contracting Process

In its final form, a Social Contract answers the question of "what we stand for" in a board/CEO partnership, and details the beliefs and behaviors that define their collective leadership. The process that I have successfully used with boards and their CEO's to create the Social Contract is straightforward and takes less than a day of the board's retreat to complete. The schedule that I usually follow is this:

- Review the strategy and strategic priorities of the business.
- Discuss the board/CEO partnership and the key challenges to achieving the business's strategy and priorities.
- Individually reflect on and list the three to five most important areas to build and maintain the board/CEO's partnership and a behavioral statement under each that would guide their work together.
- Reach a consensus on the common areas within the defining behaviors that the board/CEO will commit to as a statement of their Social Contract.
- Post the Social Contract in the boardroom and on the board agenda so it can be referred to as a standing agenda and behavioral guide.

The first two steps of the process set the stage for creating the Social Contract. The strategy and priorities of the business should be readily available for review by the board when it begins. With that in hand the board and CEO can begin to discuss the key challenges facing the company. In most instances, these will be performance or opportunity gaps they want to close. This discussion is meant to allow for a collective understanding of the strategic context and intent of the business.

The next three points in the process gather individual input and flesh out the details of the Social Contract. During the third step, each individual compiles his or her own list of priority areas along with a behavioral statement. A list that follows my five preferred behavioral standards might look like this:

1. *Commitment to values*: We are a value-driven organization whose credo defines the way we do things. Our values are clearly stated for all our stakeholders (customers, employees, shareholders, and community) to know what we stand for as an organization for them.

2. *Commitment to the stakeholders*: We know our commitment goes beyond just doing well as a business. We feel a compelling commitment to do what is right for our customers, employees, shareholders, and communities in which we work. Seeking the right balance between and among these stakeholders is the key to our overall stability and success.

3. *Commitment to risk management*: We understand that we can fail if we don't manage our risk. As much as we want to maximize our growth, we also need to constantly monitor our risk profile.

4. *Commitment to transparency*: We have a fiduciary responsibility that is supported by our commitment to transparency with our shareholders and complete honesty within our board/CEO team regarding our financial and nonfinancial matters. We respect the requirements of confidentiality where they apply but do not withhold information from our decision-making process.

5. *Commitment to coaching*: We believe in the continuous development of the board/CEO skills and abilities, and therefore commit the time and resources to learn how we can better perform in our respective roles. We view this as an obligation to our stakeholders and an investment in our future success.

Once everyone has put a list together, I ask each member of the board to read his or her individual statements while others listen for items that are similar to their own. Once everyone has read aloud, the next step is to reach a consensus on common priority areas and defining behaviors. To facilitate this process, I define a "consensus" as a selection from a list of mutually acceptable alternatives and suggest that the group combine items from individual statements and refine them as necessary, leaving out items that anyone strongly objects to. In the end, there will be a list of statements to choose from that everyone can support. With this list in front of them, I ask board members to choose their top three. After recording their individual preferences, it usually becomes clear that a select number of items receives a clear majority of support. Again, there can be some further refining and combing, but, following Miller's law, I try to hold the board to 7 ± 2. The board/CEO will then commit to these as a statement of their Social Contract.

Finally, I ask the board to post the Social Contract in the boardroom and on each member's board agenda so it can be referred to as the behavioral guide in their work together. My follow-on recommendation to the boards/CEO's I work with is that they revisit this document as needed, and at least at every scheduled retreat. I suggest, for these continued discussions of the Social Contract, that they use a facilitator who is trusted by the group. This can be either an outside consultant, as in my case, or an internal consultant knowledgeable about group dynamics and decision making and is viewed as an objective and trusted advisor.

The fundamental idea behind the Social Contract is that a board/CEO partnership cannot be sustained by good intentions alone. There must be an explicit statement of the beliefs and behaviors that are essential for the general will of the organization. With the creation of the Social Contract, a foundation is in place for a successful and productive partnership between the CEO and the board.

2

Tough Love in the Boardroom

Tough love: treating someone sternly with the intention of helping over the long run

In a successful partnership between the CEO and the board, the directors are able to assert their independence and challenge the CEO's assumptions when necessary. In the Lehman Brothers collapse it is clear that the board failed to sternly challenge Richard Fuld's assertions about the state of the business. In retrospect, he was certainly not on mission: "We are one firm, defined by our unwavering commitment to our clients, our shareholders, and each other. Our mission is to build unrivaled partnerships with and value for our clients, through the knowledge, creativity, and dedication of our people, leading to superior returns to our shareholders."[1] However, Lehman's main beliefs, as expressed in its Sustainability Principles, give us an idea of the way the CEO and board should have approached their strategic issues.

SUSTAINABILITY PRINCIPLES

Transparency and accountability. We will report regularly on the implementation of these principles.

Operations. We will aim to minimize negative environmental and social impacts of our operations.

Employees. We will engage with employees on environmental and social issues impacting our operations and business and encourage the development of innovative solutions.

Assessing risk. We will assess the environmental and social risks posed by our operations and business. We will engage with clients on critical issues (such as climate change, biodiversity loss and water scarcity).

Delivering opportunity. We will seek opportunities across our business that deliver commercial, environmental and social benefit.

Market-based solutions. We believe that market-based solutions can deliver commercially feasible environmental and social benefit. We will apply our knowledge and understanding of financial markets to develop and implement innovative environmental and social market-based solutions.

Investments. We will build our knowledge of how environmental and social issues impact business performance into advising clients, investing on clients' behalf and deploying our own capital.

Thought leadership. We will conduct research and analysis on key environmental and social issues and make the results publicly available. We will engage in public policy dialogues to contribute to the development of effective policies.

Governance. These principles are approved and owned by our Executive Committee. The Executive Committee will oversee and receive regular reports on implementation and performance.[2]

The Sustainability Principles show that the board had methods in place to address issues as a group, rather than relying solely on the CEO. Further, it had an advisory body that was focused on risk management: the Finance and Risk Committee, composed of five independent board members. This is the committee that should have challenged Fuld in 2007.

So what went wrong? The committee members did not provide an independent assessment of the company's risk but instead relied unquestioningly on Fuld's assertions. The Finance and Risk Management Committee met only twice a year in 2006 and 2007—years when Lehman's crisis was brewing, according to testimony by the Corporate Library research group to Waxman's congressional committee. "A company in this sector should have a risk management committee that is vitally involved and has a great depth of expertise," Corporate Library editor Nell Minow testified to lawmakers. "A company that had $7 billion in losses after becoming embroiled in the global credit crisis had a risk management committee that didn't understand or manage its risk."[3] And many have criticized the directors placed in that committee. Of the five, "one was a Broadway producer; one had a long and distinguished career in the US Navy; [and] one had run a Spanish-language TV station."[4]

In the years leading up to the collapse, the board failed to show Fuld the "tough love" that could have saved not only his job, but the company. "Fuld took a franchise he'd built from almost nothing, brick by brick, and then trashed it in less than two years," said Sean Egan, president and founder of Egan-Jones Ratings Co. in Haverford, Pennsylvania. "His biggest mistake was in not understanding the risks that had evolved since he was last active in debt markets. And he relied on the support of others whose interests were aligned with him."[5]

Fuld, when asked to explain his company's downfall to the congressional committee on October 6th, had no answers. "I wake up every single night," Fuld said, "thinking, 'What could I have done differently?'"[6]

Practicing Tough Love

It is clear, from the collapse of Lehman Brothers and the joint failure of Fuld and the Finance and Risk Committee, that having a statement of intent or a Social Contract in place is not always enough to ensure a successful partnership. For the board to be able to work effectively with the CEO, it must be able to ask questions, think independently, and show tough love when necessary. It is the board's responsibility to

- Know the CEO's behavioral style and leadership practices.
- Know the organization's needs (strategy, priorities, and gaps).
- Match the organization's needs with the leadership that is required.
- Look first at the CEO and then the senior team to find the correct match.
- Look elsewhere if the correct match isn't found.

The CEO's Behavioral Style and Leadership Practices

Knowing the general behavioral styles of executives can help the board provide tough love to the CEO. The idea of distinct personality types evolved out of the work of Carl Jung. Today one of the most straightforward assessments is based on the behavioral styles research of Merrill and Reid. They define four Social Styles: Driving, Expressive, Amiable, and Analytical.[7] In later chapters I discuss how these styles can be modified and expanded into leadership indices that are appropriate for CEO evaluation, and I deal more extensively with the assessment of the CEO's behavioral style and leadership practices. For now, however, let's consider how different behavioral styles can impact a company.

The CEO changeover at Coke, from Roberto Goizueta to Doug Ivester, is a classic example of the effect different behavioral styles and leadership practices can have on a company. From 1980 until his unexpected death in 1997, Goizueta created more wealth for Coke's shareholders than any other CEO in history.[8] His expressive/innovative behavior was a stark contrast to his COO, Ivester, whose analytical, process-oriented behavior was legendary within the company. In October 1997, although still in shock from losing Goizueta, Warren Buffet and the other directors were convinced that they had the right successor in Ivester, and the board meeting to appoint him lasted only 15 minutes. Given Ivester's history with the company and years of working side by side with Goizueta, the choice seemed self-evident. As *Fortune Magazine* wrote in 2000:

> For two decades Ivester had toiled away patiently inside Coke, the last ten years aiming directly at the top spot and dazzling Goizueta with his hard work and creative execution of company strategy. A onetime accountant and outside auditor, he was carefully groomed by Goizueta and put through all the paces to give him the breadth of experience he would need in marketing, in global affairs, in charm and public speaking. But for all his brilliance—and nobody doubts that Ivester is brilliant—he somehow failed to grasp the vital quality that Goizueta had in abundance: that ethereal thing called leadership.[9]

When making its decision, the board did not allow enough time to step back and ask if and how Ivester's behavioral style would align with the organization's needs. The directors apparently assumed that by going with the Number 2 to Goizueta, things would continue as in the past. However, what resulted was a mismatch of a CEO's style and the needs of an organization. It is reported that Warren Buffet and Herbert Allen, two powerful directors at the time, met with Ivester in a private meeting in Chicago and informed him that they had lost confidence in his leadership after little more than two years on the job. Ivester resigned, and Douglas Daft was appointed to the position soon after.[10]

When planning succession, the board failed to see that Goizueta was not grooming Ivester as much as he was utilizing his contrasting strengths in his leadership team. When Goizueta and Ivester worked together, Coke functioned at its peak, but a leadership gap was created when one of the players was taken away. If the board had been tougher and more deliberate in its assessment of Ivester's behavioral style and leadership practices, it might not have had to be so tough on him two years later in assessing his performance as CEO.

The Organization's Needs

If the board hopes to help its CEO in the long term, it needs to focus on the few things that will make the biggest difference in the performance of the business. There is a hierarchy of needs in every organization that is typically expressed in its strategy, priorities, and the performance and opportunity gaps—the measurable difference between the current and desired future state. In many instances, an organization will distill its needs down to a goal statement. For instance, Tyco has Board Governance Principles that clearly state its goals:

TYCO GOALS: WHAT WE SEEK TO ACHIEVE

Governance: Adhere to the highest standards of corporate governance by establishing processes and practices that promote and ensure integrity, compliance, and accountability.

Customers: Fully understand and exceed our customers' needs, wants and preferences and provide greater value to our customers than our competition.

Growth: Focus on strategies to achieve organic growth targets and deploy cash for growth and value creation.

Teamwork and Culture: Build on the company's reputation and image internally and externally while driving initiatives to ensure Tyco remains an employer of choice.

Operational Excellence: Implement best-in-class operating practices and leverage company-wide opportunities.

Financial Strength & Flexibility: Ensure that revenue, earnings per share (EPS), cash, and return on invested capital objectives are met.[11]

With these goals stated and jointly owned by the Tyco board and its CEO, the needs of the organization can be the focus of the board's work.

Matching Needs with Leadership

As was the case with Ivester at Coke, there can be a mismatch between the current needs of the organization and the leadership practices of the CEO. Ideally, this is the point where the board steps in and either shows the CEO tough love or takes more extreme action, such as removing him or her from office. Warren Buffet and Herbert Allen did the latter when they met with Ivester and delivered the board's message of no confidence.

The CEO's leadership practices must be aligned with the business in general, and the CEO must be flexible enough to change leadership style with each stage of the business. My original work linked the business cycle to critical leadership practices identified by the Kouzes and Posner research: challenge the status quo, inspire the future, enable others and model the way (see Table 2.1).[12] In a start-up or turnaround, the organization

Table 2.1.
Business Stages and CEO Practices

The Stage of the Business	CEO Practices
Low Success/Beginning Time Frame	Challenge the status quo
Rising Success/Early Time Frame	Inspire the Future
Growing Success/Middle Time Frame	Enable Others
Peak Success/Late Time Frame	Model the Way

needs a leader to challenge the status quo and build a viable business. Once the business is functional, the leader needs to provide a clear vision that inspires the future. As success is being achieved, the organization needs its leader to enable others to contribute to the growth of the business. Finally, as the organization continues to advance, the leader must model the way to continually improve the business while exploring opportunities to reinvent itself in the future.

Finding the Correct Match Internally

At Coke, the board's choice of Ivester to follow Goizueta made sense, as he was the COO under Goizueta and part of a senior team that had achieved significant success. Succession planning is built on the premise that an organization needs to have the bench strength to maintain its momentum. Boards should continually review their succession plan and determine whether their senior team matches up well with the demands of the business. Coke's board did not take the time to consider its succession options sufficiently when Goizueta died unexpectedly. Instead it immediately appointed Ivester as the obvious choice. Not only did Ivester's leadership style contrast with Goizueta's and therefore clash with Coke's needs at the time, but once appointed he did not foster a strong senior team and refused to appoint a COO, even at the board's urgings. Ivester failed as a leader, and he amplified this leadership crisis by neglecting to build an effective senior team that could complement his own style.

Richard Fuld is another example of a CEO who was not building an in-depth management team. For many years, he too refused to appoint a Number 2:

> Christopher Pettit, a longtime friend and ally of Fuld's, was forced out as chief operating officer when he balked at an executive reorganization in 1996. Six years would go by before Fuld installed another chief operating officer. The man Fuld finally appointed chief operating officer was Gregory, a trusted lieutenant who had worked at Lehman since 1974. He would make it his mission to keep Fuld's life uncomplicated by debate.[13]

Both Ivester and Fuld failed to build strong senior teams. For Coke this meant having to go outside the senior team to find a successor. The board quickly promoted Douglas Daft, who ran the company's Middle and Far East divisions, to COO and then to CEO. Had it challenged Fuld and questioned his leadership ability, the Lehman board would have found a similarly lacking senior team.

An example of a successful senior team builder is Jack Welch, the onetime CEO of GE. Welch was known for his top team, and he insisted that his colleagues share the best practices, rather than operate in isolation from one another. All the members of his senior team understood the total GE business, and this resulted in a lengthy and well-publicized succession saga prior to his retirement. James McNerney, Robert Nardelli, and Jeffrey Immelt were all considered candidates for the position. Immelt was eventually selected to succeed Welch as chairman and CEO. The trade-off for having such a strong group, however, was that the candidates who weren't chosen looked to outside opportunities to advance their careers. Nardelli became the CEO of Home Depot until his resignation in early 2007 (whereupon he was tapped by Cerberus, the private equity firm, to run Chrysler), while McNerney became CEO of 3M until he left that post to serve in the same capacity at Boeing. The positions these men went on to attests to the strength of Welch's team at GE, and this gave the board a number of options when it came time to choosing Welch's successor.

Finding the Correct Match Outside the Company

One of the toughest decisions that can be made in the boardroom is the decision to go outside the existing management team to find a CEO. However, if a board does not have the leaders to match up with the needs of its business, it must look elsewhere. The Tyco board made this decision when it selected Breen as CEO in 2002. Granted, it took a *New York Times* exposé and Manhattan district attorney indictment to initiate the former CEO's resignation and CFO's departure, but the board nonetheless made the right decision by looking elsewhere for a CEO. Rarely do we learn of the performance review by the board and its CEO unless it warrants removal or public recognition, nor should we. Tough love is based on an open and honest but confidential dialogue.

CEO Tenure and Company Performance

In fulfilling their role as the CEO's boss, boards can benefit from studies of CEO tenure and company performance. Hambrick and Fukutomi have identified five distinct seasons of a CEO's tenure, each of which is accompanied by a specific set of behaviors.[14]

According to their model, the first season of the CEO starts when he or she is hired and given a mandate from the board to advance the business. After an initial period of legitimacy building, the CEO is moved into a second season of experimentation and trying new things. If all goes well, he or she enters into a third season during which the CEO selects what works best and sticks with it. If what works endures, there is a fourth season, when actions converge to reinforce and bolster the culture of the company. That strategy becomes the "way we do things around here." Unfortunately, this convergence invites only incremental change to improve things. Eventually, the point of inflection, when success begins to shift downward from its highest point, is reached in a business cycle. This is the fifth season of the CEO: dysfunction. Hambrick and Fukutomi's model parallels the common belief about the business cycle, often referred to as the "S" curve (figure 2.1). Businesses start strong, experience a short-term decline as they try to find a winning strategy, and become more successful as they figure out what works and what doesn't. They will stick with that

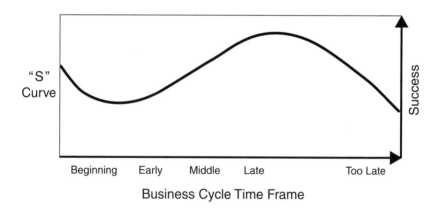

Figure 2.1.
The "S" Curve.

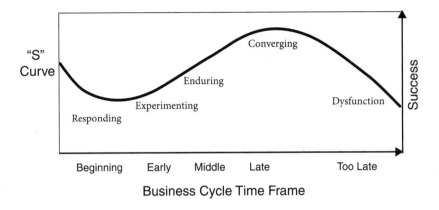

Figure 2.2.
Seasons of a CEO's Tenure and the Business Cycle. (Source: W. M. Klepper, adapted from Donald C. Hambrick and Gregory D.S. Fukutomi, "The Seasons of a CEO's Tenure," *The Academy of Management Review*, vol. 16, no. 4 (Oct. 1991), pp. 719–742.)

strategy as long as possible. However, without a parallel effort to begin a second wave, or "S" curve, dysfunction can occur—both in the leadership and in the business.

Overlaying the five seasons of the CEO's tenure on the "S" curve allows us to graph the success of the CEO at different stages in the company's growth (figure 2.2). Thus, the behaviors associated with every season can be understood as the ideal agenda for each stage of the business cycle. When the business is just getting starting, for instance, the best agenda for the CEO is to respond to the mandate from the board and to act consistently according to this mandate. At the peak of business, on the other hand, the CEO should not attempt any major changes, and should instead reinforce the strategies that have been successful in the past. If the CEO cannot make his agenda conform to the needs of the business, he'll become dysfunctional.

Many CEO's have modified their leadership style and practices to avoid collapse, and in a few instances they have achieved greatness. Jim Collins's *Good to Great* (2001) documents the most notable of these companies. However, without the CEO and company continually adapting to changing conditions, dysfunction can result. Collins's recent book, *How the Mighty Fall*, paints the picture of these stages of decline, depicted on an

"S" curve.[15] In these economic times, there are references to "L," "W," and even "√" curves, but the "S" curve is an accepted model for explaining the business cycle time frame. CEO's can join a company at any point in the business cycle, and thus the seasons of the CEO do not necessarily happen chronologically. Further, a flexible CEO can modify his or her leadership style and avoid dysfunction.

Looking back, it is clear that there were signs of dysfunction on Fuld's part before Lehman's collapse. He was underpowered to figure out the right risk/reward ratios and make the right decisions, and he took relatively few actions to confront the risk profile of the firm. "A CEO needs good managers reporting to him to figure out the right risk-reward ratios and make the right decisions. Increasingly, Fuld wasn't getting good dope. He became isolated in recent years, people familiar with the firm's operations said. He countenanced little debate and delegated more responsibility to Joseph M. Gregory, 56, who became president and chief operating officer in 2004."[16] The board must address these realities with tough love or share in the responsibility for the company and CEO becoming dysfunctional. In the case of Lehman, it is legitimate to ask, "What was the board doing to confront the CEO's dysfunction?" As some have concluded, it was not doing enough:

> As the world nervously awaits the effects of the unprecedented Lehman Brothers liquidation, one can't help but wonder how and why this board let its long-time chairman and patron, Richard Fuld Jr., cling to both hope and power. Perhaps it was because Mr. Fuld wanted it that way. Over the years, Mr. Fuld had become the living embodiment of the securities firm, creating a top-down culture that sometimes had a military feel to it. Most mornings, Mr. Fuld rode alone in an elevator up to his executive suite. His colleagues simply call him "The Chairman."
>
> And it is telling that press accounts of Lehman's capital-raising efforts focused entirely on the efforts of Mr. Fuld, and make nary a mention of the 10 other members of Lehman's board.[17]

Uncertainties of Business Cycles: JetBlue

The problem with business cycles is that, given their inherent uncertainties, it can be difficult to predict what the next phase in the cycle will be.

The "S" curve will emerge over time, but in the short term it can be hard for a company to gauge where it is situated. The JetBlue board, under the direction of its founder, David Neeleman, found itself in these uncertain conditions. When board members realized their company was faltering, they were able to show tough love and shift their leadership, even when it was the founder who needed to be swapped out.

JetBlue Airways was founded in 1999 with the premise of "bringing humanity back to air travel."[18] Neeleman had had success in the business before—he co-founded his first airline, Morris Air, when he was only twenty-five, and later sold it to Southwest Airlines, the leading low-cost carrier (LCC) in the industry. He'd also served for three years as the CEO of Open Skies, the company that helped develop e-ticket technology. When JetBlue opened for business in 2000, Neeleman distinguished it from other airlines by offering such perks as seatback television, comfortable seating, and blue corn chips. In the company's own words: "No exorbitant airfares, no cattle-train mentality, no hassles. In their place, add simplicity, friendly people, technology, design, and entertainment. JetBlue is a different kind of airline . . . younger, fresher, and more innovative. We're looking at creative ways to reduce the hassles of flying and simplify the travel experience."[19]

Despite its emphasis on how it differed from existing airlines, JetBlue also emulated some of the most successful features of Southwest Airlines, such as investment in human resources.[20] This mix of innovation and emulation worked. At a time when big airlines were losing money, JetBlue continued to post profits, and the forty-year-old Neeleman became an icon in the airline industry. Delta and United soon launched their own LCCs to compete with the budding airline.

But, even given its initial success, the question remained: Could the fledgling company really "fly" in such a difficult industry? As Warren Buffet once remarked, if capitalists had been present at Kitty Hawk when the Wright brothers' plane first took off, they should have shot it down. When JetBlue entered the market, the U.S. airline industry faced daunting problems. Fuel costs were high, and even airlines that had made successful hedges against these higher costs, like Southwest, were straining under the pressure. Coupled with that were the large fixed costs—namely, aircraft—and a consistently competitive environment. Despite these industry difficulties, JetBlue's position as a second-tier airline was advantageous. "The second tier, composed of newer airlines that never put in place huge legacy costs before deregulation unleashed price competition, limits the top tier's ability to pass along costs to customers."[21] JetBlue seemed to have the right business plan to succeed in a difficult market.

Initially flying only between New York and Florida, the airline expanded to California, Utah, and Vermont during its first few months of business, and celebrated its millionth flyer before its one-year anniversary. It launched international service in 2004 and continued to expand its domestic service. However, in 2005, JetBlue began to falter under the weight of increased fuel prices and its own rapid expansion. Discussing the full-year results in 2005, Neeleman said, "We are very disappointed in our performance this quarter as we continued to feel the effects of record-high fuel prices and a tough revenue environment, compounded by the impact of Hurricane Wilma and the residual effects of Hurricanes Katrina and Rita. Although we saw a 7.4% increase in revenue per available seat mile (RASM) in the face of 25% capacity growth, it was not nearly enough to offset the impact of high fuel costs."[22]

JetBlue continued to lose money in 2006, and just as business was picking up in 2007, the East Coast was hit by a paralyzing snowstorm over Valentine's Day weekend. Unlike other airlines, JetBlue did not heed weather warnings and did not cancel flights until it was too late. In a business disaster that the press dubbed the "Valentine Massacre," thousands of customers were stranded on planes and in airports, with some customers stuck at JFK for days. In response, the company released a press report stating: "JetBlue apologizes to customers who were impacted by the ice storm at our home base of operations in New York, specifically at John F. Kennedy International Airport," and gave a full refund and a free round trip to any customer kept onboard planes for more than three hours.[23] More candidly, spokeswoman Jenny Dervin said, "We ran into an operational death spiral. We let our customers down, and we're terribly sorry it happened."[24]

JetBlue's initial rise and subsequent fall are a good illustration of the uncertainties of the business cycle, and this case provides a good platform for exploring both how a CEO's style impacts the company and how "tough love" from the board can be used when this style is no longer working.

Neeleman, with one successful airline behind him and the drive to get companies started, was obviously in his element during JetBlue's infant years, but he was also cognizant that the company required flexibility from its leader as it expanded in 2006 and 2007. I heard Neeleman describe his leadership capabilities in his own words during a lecture for a group of MBA students in the Marketing Club at Columbia Business School on

January 23, 2007. He was very forthcoming about his leadership style and its accompanying strengths and weaknesses. He was well aware of the realities facing JetBlue at that point. Although his business had gotten through its start-up phase and was starting to build momentum, he recognized that 2005 had been a point of inflection. Efficiency and cash flow became the priority when the company started to falter, and it was important to know the "numbers" on an hour-by-hour basis so that JetBlue could change fares as needed, rather than staying locked into a standard rate structure. Although Neeleman had the right entrepreneurial, innovative style and industry know-how to get the business started, he knew he wasn't the right person to lead a detail-oriented intervention. Operational efficiency is more the diet of an analytical style, a process person tied to an operational drive that thrives in the tactical, and the company changed its revenue management leadership to address this. However, despite his awareness of his own shortfalls as a leader, Neeleman's innovative spirit shone through during the lecture, and he excitedly discussed such new plans for the company as letting the customer buy the middle seat and spread out during coast-to-coast flights.

As it turned out, Neeleman would have little time to develop these ideas. On May 10, 2007, three months after the Valentine's weekend debacle, JetBlue announced the appointment of Dave Barger to the position of chief executive officer, replacing Neeleman immediately, while retaining his responsibilities as president. "This is a natural evolution of our leadership structure as JetBlue continues to grow," Neeleman said. "As Chairman of the Board of Directors, I will focus on developing JetBlue's long-term vision and strategy and how we can continue to be a preferred product in a commodity business."[25]

The board also realized that Neeleman's leadership style no longer fit with the needs of the company, and showed the tough love necessary to get the business back on track. The board confronted Neeleman after the Valentine Massacre and they jointly arrived at the decision to replace him as chief executive. Circumstances are not ideal when a board assesses its CEO at a time of crisis, and it is an even greater challenge when the founder is at the helm. Indeed, from my discussions with people involved with the company at the time, the members of the board all had considerable admiration for Neeleman, and the fact that he knew of his shortfalls as a leader indicates that he was in communication with his board about what kind of leadership style was best for the company. However, after the events in February, it must have become clear that despite their amiability toward and regard for him, Neeleman had to be replaced. This is an example of tough love in action. The positive results of this change in leadership were immediately apparent, with the company reporting a net income of $18 million in 2007 compared with a net loss of $1 million in 2006.[26] This was the first profitable year the company had had since 2004. As Dave Barger reported: "Although soaring fuel prices contributed to our fourth-quarter loss, we believe we are well positioned as we move into 2008 with a strong brand, superior product and solid financial position."[27]

At this writing, JetBlue has been affirmed as a unique offering in the airline industry, receiving top honors in three categories in the 2008 Zagat Airline Survey: "Best Large Domestic Airline" for economy-class seating, "Best Inflight Entertainment" for domestic flights, and "Most Eco-Friendly" airline. In 2009, the company was named the "Top Low Cost Airline for Customer Satisfaction" by J. D. Power and Associates. Southwest Airlines continues to be the gold standard of LCCs, but JetBlue has made its mark through its innovative and unique offerings to its customers. As one frequent flyer of JetBlue, I hope they make it.

And, as a follower of the creative leadership of David Neeleman, I look forward to watching his career in the airline industry develop. Although he stayed with JetBlue for a year as chairman of the board, on April 8, 2008, he notified the Corporate Governance and Nominating Committee that he would not be standing for reelection at the annual meeting. He was leaving to do what he'd done successfully twice before—found an airline. In December 2008, he launched the Brazilian domestic airline Azul, which had already captured 5% of the market by July 2009. The JetBlue board, by showing Neeleman tough love when the company was faltering, both regained success for the company and freed Neeleman to pursue other endeavors.

The airline business is a very difficult one under any circumstances, and the board must constantly assess and adjust its leadership in order to survive. Finding the right partnership between the board and its CEO is central to a company's success. When JetBlue was in a period of growth, it was a perfect match for David Neeleman's entrepreneurial style, but as the business expanded, a more operationally efficient leader was needed. It took a crisis to make the change, but the change was made.

How is a board to know when this change needs to happen? The best advice is to assume your business is always at the point of inflection and to be prepared to make a shift in practices and encourage your CEO to do the same. The following chapters offer additional guidance. Because a CEO's leadership style is so central to a company's success, boards can benefit from those who study CEO tenure and company performance as well as the requisite leadership behaviors to achieve success at the various stages in the life cycle of their business. If the board doesn't address these realities with the appropriate amount of tough love, the company and CEO can become dysfunctional.

3

Why the Right Partnership Matters

Point of Inflection: A moment of dramatic change, especially in the development of a company, industry, or market.

In the opening chapter, the Social Contract—a clear set of behavioral statements willingly subscribed to by the board and CEO—was prescribed to strengthen and maintain the partnership between these parties. In chapter 2, tough love was presented as a requirement to make this partnership work. These two elements are crucial to a company's survival. Every board needs to face the reality that business cycles are unavoidable and uncertain, and the board and CEO must be willing to work collectively to meet the challenge of changing conditions—points of inflection.

Leadership Style

As was depicted in table 2.1, each stage of the business cycle requires a specific leadership practice. And, as was depicted in figure 2.2, each stage requires a specific agenda. The CEO's practices and agenda, which describe what the CEO *does*, are important, but *how* the CEO carries them out and the leadership style used can make the difference between success and failure.

My work with leadership styles draws from the "Social Styles," developed by TRACOM, the company founded by Merrill and Reid. In the

1980s, I taught the Social Styles material in an MBA course with Martha Stodt, a fellow faculty member from Columbia's Teachers College. The course was called Managing Interpersonal and Group Dynamics; today it would be called Social Intelligence. We had previously published a book and designed and developed workshops along the same theme. When I moved to Columbia Business School from my executive leadership role at the College of New Jersey in 1996, I began to focus my Executive Education teaching more on executive leadership, but I continued to apply the Social Styles material in that work. The Klepper Leadership Model that was published in Capon's *Key Account Management* was one of the first iterations of that application.[1] More recently, my article "What CEOs Have Yet to Learn," published in *Effective Executive*, reports on my research on the leadership practices of CEO's. The information presented in this chapter is the natural evolution of that research and the research of others (D. C. Hambrick and G. Fukutomi; J. M. Kouzes and B. Z. Posner). It illustrates my continued application of the Social Styles material of Merrill and Reid to CEO and board leadership strategies.

I've worked with executives over the last 20 years in the application of this Social Style Model to leadership. First, the executive takes a Social Style assessment, which yields a description of how assertive and how responsive a person is. One can both self-assess and have others provide this assessment (a "360" assessment). The Social Style Model is based on the assertive and responsive dimensions that are measured by this assessment (figure 3.1):

- Assertiveness—the degree to which people see themselves as tending to "ask" (ask assertive) or as tending to "tell" (tell assertive) in their interactions with others.
- Responsiveness—the degree to which people see themselves as tending to "control" (keep feelings and emotions inside) or "emote" (outwardly display feelings and emotions with others).

Combining these dimensions produces a fourfold Social Style scheme (figure 3.2):

- Driving—tell assertive/control;
- Expressive—tell assertive/emote;
- Amiable—ask assertive/emote;
- Analytical—ask assertive/control.

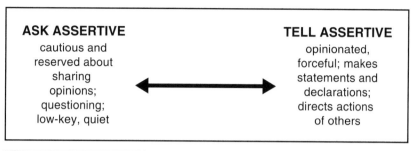

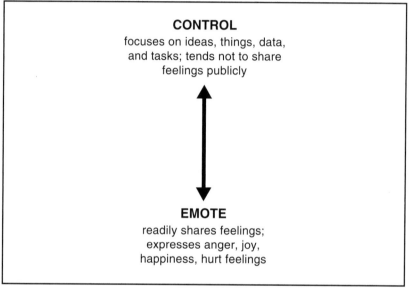

Figure 3.1.
Assertiveness and Responsiveness. (Source: Improving Personal Effectiveness with Versatility, © The TRACOM Corporation 2007. SOCIAL STYLE and TRACOM are trademarks of The TRACOM Corporation. Visit www.socialstyle.com to learn more.)

As Capon's *Key Account Management* explains, a Social Style is

the most persistent, socially evident, pattern of behavior that a person demonstrated to others. All social styles have value, but people interact differently with one another based on these observable, repetitive patterns of behavior. The driver is primarily assertive, serious and makes an effort to tell people what they think and require. The

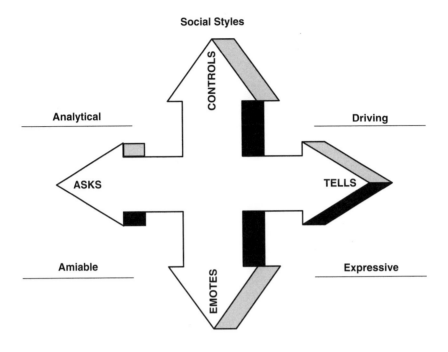

Figure 3.2.
Social Styles Scheme. (Source: Improving Personal Effectiveness with Versatility, © The TRACOM Corporation 2007. SOCIAL STYLE and TRACOM are trademarks of The TRACOM Corporation. Visit www.socialstyle.com to learn more.)

expressive is more willing to make their feelings public and is decisive and forceful. The amiable displays feelings openly, but is less assertive and more interested in being agreeable and cooperative. The analytical person tends to ask questions, gather facts, and study data seriously.[2]

I have expanded on this research to define the leadership styles appropriate to various business stages. Combining the CEO agenda and practices from chapter 2 with the CEO style and situating all these in terms of the business cycle can give us a complete idea of the CEO's leadership requirements (table 3.1).

An understanding of each style's need, orientation, and response to stress in interactions with others can provide additional understanding of a CEO's leadership style. However, although each individual may tend

Table 3.1.
The CEO's Leadership Requirements

The Business Cycle	CEO Agenda	CEO Practices	CEO Style
Low Success/Beginning Time Frame	Responding to a mandate to change	Challenge the status quo	Driver
Rising Success/Early Time Frame	Experimenting; trying new things	Inspire the Future	Expressive
Growing Success/Middle Time Frame	Enduring; doing what works	Enable Others	Amiable
Peak Success/Late Time Frame	Converging on the status quo	Model the Way	Analytical

naturally toward a certain style, this does not mean that leadership styles are fixed. Most CEO's have one primary style and one or more secondary styles that they can draw on when necessary. Since businesses are constantly changing, the most successful CEO's can modify their leadership styles to suit their company's needs. Jack Welch, onetime CEO of GE, is a prime example of a versatile leader. As I present each style, I will discuss how and when Welch adopted it in his leadership of the company, and I will offer examples of other CEO's whose leadership styles have or have not worked for their companies.

Driver Leadership

CEO's with a Driver style need to see results from their work with others, and they approach work from an "action" orientation. Driver-type leaders work effectively when these conditions exist, but if they are not seeing results from their actions, they will take control until things change.

Driver behavior is most helpful during a downturn in a business cycle—a "trough," as it is often called—such as at the start of Jack Welch's tenure as CEO at GE. Welch made drastic changes to the company as soon as he arrived, downsizing from 411,000 employees at the end of 1980 to 299,000 at the end of 1985. These major cuts earned him the nickname

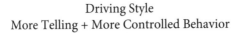

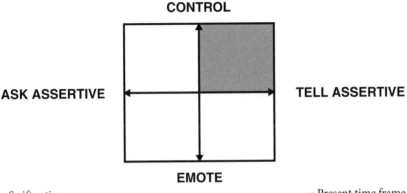

Driving Style
More Telling + More Controlled Behavior

CONTROL

ASK ASSERTIVE   **TELL ASSERTIVE**

EMOTE

- Swift action
- Maximum effort to control
- Minimum concern for caution in relationships

- Present time frame
- Direct action
- Tends to avoid inaction

Figure 3.3.
Driver Leadership. (Source: Improving Personal Effectiveness with Versatility, © The TRACOM Corporation 2007. SOCIAL STYLE and TRACOM are trademarks of The TRACOM Corporation. Visit www.socialstyle.com to learn more.)

"Neutron Jack." Just like a neutron bomb, which damages people but not buildings, Welch left the infrastructure of GE intact but eliminated many of the jobs. A closer look at the Driver style can provide a fuller understanding of Welch's leadership practices and of why he was so adept at taking action and achieving results (figure 3.3).

When Welch became CEO he knew that he couldn't wait for change to happen on its own. He acted appropriately as a new CEO, challenging the status quo and making dramatic cuts across the board. By 1982, Welch had gutted the leadership team of his predecessor, Reginald Jones. And he went to extreme measures to ensure that the company ran with maximum efficiency, infamously firing the bottom 10 percent of his managers every year. Known for his candor, Welch did not apologize for this practice, and wrote in his book *Winning:* "As for the bottom 10 percent in differentiation, there is no sugarcoating this—they have to go."[3]

Expressive Leadership

CEO's with an Expressive style need approval of their vision for the future, and they have a "spontaneous" orientation to their work. To put it succinctly—they trust their gut. I'm not surprised that Welch chose *Straight from the Gut* as the title of his first book. It was well known that he confronted poor performance when he saw it, and this is the prototypical reaction to stress by an Expressive. If businesses couldn't achieve the goals he set for them, Jack would "close, fix, or sell" them. This style, diagrammed in figure 3.4, was used by Welch during the rising success of GE. It is characterized by a willingness to experiment and try new things.

GE came out of its trough during Welch's early tenure, and under him annual revenues grew from $27 billion in 1980 to almost $130 billion in 2000. As the company grew, Welch took on the qualities of an Expressive leader, and he used these strategies in concert with his characteristic Driver style. He was able to challenge the status quo through his Driver

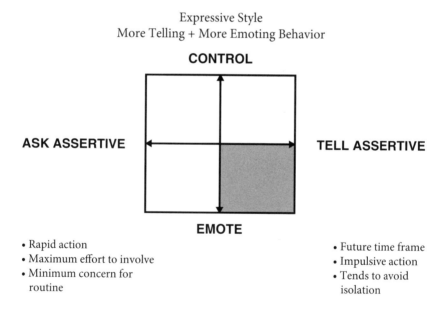

Figure 3.4.
Expressive Leadership. (Source: Improving Personal Effectiveness with Versatility, © The TRACOM Corporation 2007. SOCIAL STYLE and TRACOM are trademarks of The TRACOM Corporation. Visit www.socialstyle.com to learn more.)

behavior, but also to inspire others through his Expressive behavior. The two styles worked well for him as he responded to the mandate of change from the board and the need to redefine the future of GE. The ability to look toward the future is another hallmark of an Expressive leader, and Welch demonstrated his future-oriented mindset when he acquired NBC in 1986. In 1919, GE founded RCA, which grew into an industrial giant. It returned to its media roots through this acquisition.

However, along with these positive Expressive traits, Welch also showed some of the negative ones. For instance, some view GE's acquisition of Kidder as an impulse buy. The company was involved in a trading scandal shortly after being acquired by GE and was quietly sold off to PaineWebber in 1994. Another downside to an Expressive leadership style is a short attention span when it comes to routine activities. This explains why many entrepreneurs populate this style—they would rather move on to the next big idea than deal with the nitty-gritty of seeing a project through. David Neeleman, JetBlue's founding CEO, is an example of this style in action. Such leaders can become bored with process improvement as their daily diet. Nonetheless, Jack Welch understood that attending to routine matters was necessary, and he sought outside resources to support these efforts. In 1995, for instance, Welch adopted Motorola's Six Sigma quality program. If you have a mature product line, you can reap greater return from your portfolio by manufacturing and delivering products in the most efficient and effective way possible. Six Sigma quality is a proven practice to provide efficient and effective processes and resultant outcomes.

Ed Kangas, whom I observed during my work with Deloitte beginning in the mid-1990s, is a prototypical Expressive leader. As the global head of Deloitte Touche Tohmatsu (DTT), he inspired his partners to embrace the vision of seamless global service for its clients—then among the "big eight" firms, today among the "big four" still standing.

Amiable Leadership

CEO's with an Amiable style seek a sense of personal security in their work with others. Their leadership is oriented around the quality of their relationships with those being led. This leadership style is most effective in a period of growing success, a time when the business is enduring and a culture is being established based on "what works for us" (figure 3.5).

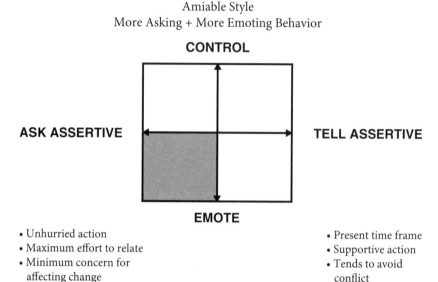

Amiable Style
More Asking + More Emoting Behavior

- Unhurried action
- Maximum effort to relate
- Minimum concern for affecting change

- Present time frame
- Supportive action
- Tends to avoid conflict

Figure 3.5.
Amiable Leadership. (Source: Improving Personal Effectiveness with Versatility, © The TRACOM Corporation 2007. SOCIAL STYLE and TRACOM are trademarks of The TRACOM Corporation. Visit www.socialstyle.com to learn more.)

Jack Welch was no Amiable leader, but he surrounded himself with Amiable personalities who shared his vision and goals for the GE businesses. Welch's appreciation for Amiable leadership was most apparent in his commitment to GE's Leadership Development Center at Crotonville, renamed the John F. Welch Leadership Development Center after he retired. There was a concerted effort to build quality relationships between and among the managers of GE, and the Amiable leaders at Crotonville allowed GE managers to interact and learn the "GE way of doing things" in an unhurried, supportive, and secure environment. Welch continued to be the agent of change, but at Crotonville managers were given the space to improve the processes for implementing this change. During his tenure, Welch routinely visited Crotonville to interact with the managers. (The only year he didn't was in 1995, when he was recovering from triple bypass surgery.)

Welch used Crotonville and the Amiable leadership within the Learning Center to reinforce his strong interest in shareholder value. He knew that this was the way that GE would endure and that Crotonville was where values like this could be ensured. Today GE's Chief Learning Officer Bob Corcoran says, "Crotonville is embedded in the GE culture and the GE values. All of our major change initiatives—cultural change and business change processes—have either originated at Crotonville as a result of best practice assessments and evaluations or executive leadership summits, or have been broadcast, trained, amplified or rolled out with Crotonville as the change agent. We owe to our shareholders the absolute best management team we can field."[4]

The Amiable leadership style has achieved even more credence since Jim Collins completed his work on "Good to Great" companies. Along a spectrum from "Highly Capable Individual" to "Level 5 Leaders," he classed as "Level 5 Leaders" those CEO's who had, over time, built strong cultures and leveraged a set of beliefs and behaviors that drove their organization's success. David Neeleman had this Amiable style in his overall leadership package as CEO of JetBlue. Although he was primarily an Expressive leader, as are most entrepreneurs, he believed that innovation plus a service culture was JetBlue's competitive advantage. Another example of an Amiable leader is GE's current CEO, Jeff Immelt, who recently confirmed to me in a conversation that this was his style and that it was in contrast to Jack Welch's Driving style. He is continuing to build the GE culture but suffers from the comparison with his predecessor's unprecedented results.

Analytical Leadership

CEO's with an Analytical style are strongly driven to "get it right," and their orientation is to "think things through." Analytical leaders look for trends in the data in order to predict outcomes, and this makes them more cautious and deliberate in their actions. As a result, their efforts are directed at organizing for success. Due diligence is the hallmark of their work and their singular mission is to "discover truth" and to maintain the peak performance of the business. Since facts rule, relationships are not a major consideration (figure 3.6).

Continuous improvement is the focus of the analytical CEO. Jack Welch showed this analytical quality to his leadership in his adoption of Motorola's Six Sigma quality program. He knew that GE's businesses had reached the number 1 or number 2 position in their fields, but to keep them there he

Analytical Style
More Asking + More Controlled Behavior

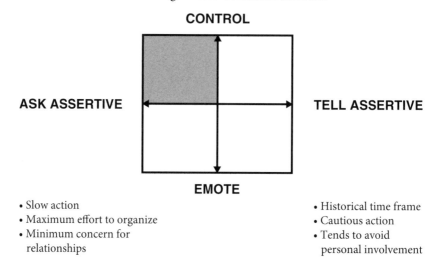

- Slow action
- Maximum effort to organize
- Minimum concern for
  relationships

- Historical time frame
- Cautious action
- Tends to avoid
  personal involvement

Figure 3.6.
Analytical Leadership. (Source: Improving Personal Effectiveness with Versatility,
© The TRACOM Corporation 2007. SOCIAL STYLE and TRACOM are trademarks
of The TRACOM Corporation. Visit www.socialstyle.com to learn more.)

needed to make efficiency and effectivity top priorities. Larry Bossidy, whom Welch chose to lead his Six Sigma program, went on to become a successful analytical CEO himself. Bossidy's book *Execution* tells how he transformed Allied Signal into one of the world's most admired companies, whose success was characterized by an intense focus on growth and the Six Sigma–driven productivity that he became known for while at GE.[5]

Jack Welch increased his versatility as a leader by surrounding himself with the right people for the needs of GE. Another paradigmatic analytic is P&G's CEO, A. G. Lafley. Before his retirement in July of 2009, I observed him during a three-day workshop at the Army Work College and can attest to his analytical skills. This style is a perfect match for P&G's drive for continuous improvement of its product offerings.

Analytical leaders are at their best at the peak of success on the business cycle. Unfortunately, this can also be the point of inflection for the business. As noted in chapter 1, Coke's Doug Ivester was known as a strong Analytical leader, but his inability to adopt any other styles of leadership made him an ineffectual CEO. His board had turned to him after the untimely death of Roberto Goizueta, an Expressive leader, presumably with the idea that hiring the existing number 2 would help business continue as usual. However, the contrasting styles of the CEO's created too stark a transition for the business and the board. Ivester led the business as he had when he was COO under Goizueta—using an Analytical style that complemented, but was not a substitute for, Goizueta's leadership.

In some cases, however, this transition from one type of CEO to another is exactly what a company needs. When Driving/Expressive leaders run into problems with their transformational strategies and the business is failing, Analytical leaders, with their emphasis on incremental change, are often sought out by the board. A struggling business can be turned around by someone who understands the numbers and knows the trends of the business and industry.

Rather than demand an abrupt change in the leadership style of the CEO, another option the board has is to hire consulting agencies to do the analytical thinking for them. This is often a more realistic option than tackling the problem themselves, as it is rare that a CEO and board have time to collectively engage in the situational analysis that is required to assess and redefine business strategy. The advantage of an outside consultancy is that it is removed from the organization's personal relationships and can offer an objective assessment of the current state. However, the downside is that the CEO and board don't do any of the strategic thinking themselves, and thus it can be difficult for them to fully understand the proposed strategic changes. In a recent *Agenda* article, I called for more involvement of board members and the CEO with these consultancies while situation analysis is occurring. "When boards and managements haven't gone through the hard work of thinking strategically, they can't do the process of deciding strategically. There are just no shortcuts."[6]

The Right Alignment, the Right Partnership

These four leadership styles, with their corresponding CEO practices and agenda, can all be charted on the business cycle. This chart, which I've dubbed the Integrated Leadership Model (ILM), shows the interplay of all the elements a board must consider in aligning its CEO with the needs of the business (figure 3.7).

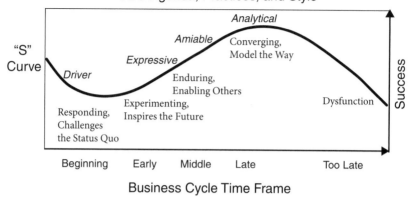

Figure 3.7.
The Integrated Leadership Model. (All Rights Reserved, William Klepper, 2009.)

To use the ILM, the first question a board must ask itself is, "Where is the business?" Is it a start-up? Is it in a trough and in need of a turn-around? Is it creating new products or services, experimenting with new ways of doing things? Is it a leader in the industry, at its peak performance and prospering by following a successful strategy? Is it seeking to get even better at what it does—or is it destined to become dysfunctional? At each one of these points on the "S" curve the board should assess its CEO's practices, agenda, and leadership style to determine if they are aligned with the company's current situation.

Often the most helpful thing a CEO can do is manage change, so that the company can adapt to the ever-changing business cycle. The work of Michael Beer, Warner Burke, and others reinforces a formula for this process.[7] To manage change a leader needs to create **D**issatisfaction with the current state, offer a **V**ision of the future and a **P**rocess to get there in order to overcome the natural resistance to **C**hange: $D \times V \times P > C$.[8] The Driver leader is strongest at challenging the status quo, thus creating dissatisfaction. The Expressive leader's strength is to inspire the future with a compelling vision. The Analytical leader is best at modeling the way by defining a process for achieving the vision. The Amiable leader has the desire to enable others during the change process that lowers their natural resistance to change. The board must understand both its CEO's leadership style and the company's point on the business cycle if it is to help the CEO manage change.

In the transition from Goizueta to Ivester at Coke, the board should have assessed where the company was in the business cycle before hiring a CEO with a leadership style so dramatically different from that of his predecessor. I suspect they didn't have the privilege of time to make that assessment. However, had that assessment occurred, it would most probably have included a discussion of Coke's experimentation with the brand (The New Coke) and its position as the leader in the industry. According to my model, then, an Amiable leader would have made for a successful transition. People at Coke were feeling disoriented and insecure about the future of Coke after the death of Goizueta, and it was a time to put a priority on relationships and stability.

JetBlue's changeover from David Neeleman to Dave Barger is an example of a successful assessment and transition to a new type of leader. During the start-up phase, Neeleman was the ideal leader for the job. He was an Expressive leader, with the added advantage of an Amiable subset, and he believed that innovation and a service culture would help JetBlue compete with the industry's leader, Southwest Airlines. However, when business started to fail and especially after the Valentine Massacre, the board had to ask whether it had reached a point of inflection and needed a change in leadership. By appointing Dave Barger to the position of CEO, the board moved toward a more Analytical Driving leadership style for the company, appropriate when a business needs to be turned around. However, had the board done a more regular and honest assessment of how its leadership aligned with the needs of the business, it might have been able to make productive changes to leadership and avoid the Valentine Massacre completely.

Recently, I had a discussion with John Mowell about CEO transitions. Mowell is the board chairman of EMS Technologies, a company that designs and manufactures innovative wireless, satellite, and defense solutions. He has applied this integrated leadership model to his company's succession planning and CEO choice, and he affirms from his experience that there are seasons of a CEO's tenure and that they can be either aligned or misaligned with the needs of the organization. EMS's recent success is a testament to the board's ability to achieve the right partnership by reexamining its CEO's capability at each stage of its business life cycle. EMS had experienced one downturn in 2005 from its high in 2004 and experienced yet another in 2006, just when business seemed to be picking up.

The board started to look for a CEO whose leadership agenda, practices, and style could confront these fluctuations in its business cycle. As a result, Paul Domorski was brought in to replace Alfred G. Hansen, CEO since 2001. EMS's rise in performance through 2007 confirmed that Domorski had the leadership style needed to turn around the business. The company concluded 2007 with the healthiest cash balance in its 40-year history, and was named one of *Forbes Magazine*'s Best Small Companies in 2007.

The lesson learned from each of these case studies is that boards have something to learn from those who study the tenure, performance, and ideal leadership behaviors of CEO's for each stage of the business. Boards can foster the right partnership between their CEO and their business by using the Integrated Leadership Model I've proposed. However, if this model is adopted too late in a CEO's tenure, it can be difficult to make productive changes. Note that at the furthest extension of the business cycle is a point at which it is too late to align the leadership with the needs of the business. In the earlier work that I cited on the seasons of a CEO, the fifth and final stage is a state of dysfunction. The CEO's take relatively few actions to address the performance of the business and their outside interests increase. This is the point at which the CEO becomes obsolete and must be removed—tough love in the boardroom.

However, this bleak outcome is not the only possibility. CEO's can reinvent themselves when they are at that point of inflection by starting a second wave of the "S" curve, which acts as a new beginning for the business before it moves into decline. When business is at its peak, this is the time to revisit the assumptions that support the existing business model and ask if the situation those assumptions were based on has changed. At this point, it is still possible to renew the business model and reexamine the way things are done in the business. The ideal leader to "restart" the business is one with both an Analytical style, to make sense of the changing conditions, and a Driving style, to challenge the status quo and embrace the change that is needed. If CEO's don't want to become obsolete, they need to modify their leadership style when it is required, or surround themselves with a leadership team with the qualities they lack.

4

Leadership Metrics

What gets measured gets done, what gets rewarded
gets done repeatedly.

As I discussed in chapter 3, each stage on the "S" curve demands a different set of leadership behaviors of the CEO. To gain a complete measure of
what matters and what works in their partnership with the CEO, board
directors need to go beyond the hard metrics of business performance
[return on assets (ROA), return on equity (ROE), return on investment
(ROI), and so on] to the soft metrics of a CEO's leadership. "Soft metrics"
is a term for intangible indicators used to value a start-up company, but
the definition has been expanded to apply to business in general—intangible
assets that don't appear on the balance sheet. It includes factors such
as integrity, leadership, developing internal candidates, communication
skills, and strategic thinking. An assessment of a CEO's leadership behaviors as observed by others—directors, direct reports, customers, and
others—is the starting point for measuring the strength of the CEO's leadership. This assessment process is standard procedure, and a number of
instruments are available that offer this feedback. The CEO assessment
that many companies use is exhibited in Charan's *Boards That Deliver* and
includes segments on company performance, leadership of the organization, team building and management succession, leadership of external
constituencies, and leadership of the board (if the CEO is also chair).[1] The

CEO would also self-assess on the same set of indices, so that the board can identify any misalignments or gaps between the self-assessment of the CEO and the assessment of the board and others.

Measuring Leadership Practices

In most CEO assessment instruments, the questions in the leadership section revolve around strategy, confronting external realities, transforming the organization, and focusing on the right issues and execution. However, Columbia Executive Education has provided feedback to hundreds of executives using a more comprehensive feedback instrument. Titled the Leadership Compass Inventory, it was developed by Michael Fenlon while he was on the Executive Education faculty at Columbia Business School, in collaboration with Joel Brockner. It serves as an assessment and action planning tool for CEO's.[2] The 65-item multirater (360-degree) instrument provides data in four essential dimensions of leadership:

1. *Leading the Organization:* These scales assess effectiveness in providing organizational direction and creating focus on key priorities, promoting innovation and strategic thinking, leading change, decision making, building community, and communicating with impact.

2. *Leading Groups:* These scales assess effectiveness in building teams, networks, and communities. Specific issues include coordinating the work of teams as well as managing team relationships, and building and utilizing networks both within and outside of the organization.

3. *Leading as a Coach:* These scales assess interpersonal skills, such as feedback, setting goals, confronting performance problems, recognizing and rewarding outstanding performance, developing leadership skills in others, and valuing diverse opinions, styles, and cultures.

4. *Leading as a Person:* These scales assess the foundational attributes of leadership, such as demonstrating confidence, projecting energy and enthusiasm, exhibiting openness to feedback and disagreement, self-awareness of personal strengths and weaknesses, and leading by example.[3]

I conducted a study of CEO's who had completed the Leadership Compass over a period of 6 years (2001–2006) and put together a group profile that included a set of practices of those CEO's. This study appeared in the article "What Effective CEO's Have Yet to Learn,"[4] and was prompted by Peter Drucker's June 2004 article "What Makes an Effective Executive."[5] As I read through his list, my thoughts immediately went to my work with the executives who had participated in Columbia Business School's Executive Education programs. The practices that Drucker highlighted were very similar to the effective practices found within the Leadership Compass, which I had used with the participants of my program (table 4.1).

What struck me, however, was that approaching the question of effectiveness in terms of this list of positives was only one side of the coin, and in

Table 4.1.
Drucker's and Columbia's Practices of Effective Executives

Drucker's Practices of Effective Executives	Columbia's Practices of Effective CEOs
A. Gathering Knowledge	
They asked, "What needs to be done?"	Shows enthusiasm for the work we do.
They asked, "What is right for the enterprise?"	Demonstrates strong personal commitment to high standards of excellence.
B. Converting Knowledge into Effective Decisions	
They developed action plans.	Demonstrates perseverance in achieving goals.
They took responsibility for decisions.	Behaves consistently with own words and standards.
They took responsibility for communicating.	Is accessible and approachable for talking about issues or concerns.
They were focused on opportunities rather than on problems.	Demonstrates calm and stamina under stressful circumstances.
C. Ensuring the Whole Organization Felt Responsible and Accountable	
They ran productive meetings.	Effectively uses his/her network of relationships inside the organization.
They thought and said "we" rather than "I."	Demonstrates respect for others.

my study I wanted to look at the flip side. The Drucker and Columbia practices tell us what effective executives most often *have*, but my study focused instead on the practices that effective executives *lack*. Boards should be on the lookout from the start for things that CEO's could be doing better— tough love thinking early about not just the hard metrics of the business but the soft metrics of a CEO's leadership. From the group profile data of the CEO's in my study, I've identified six practices that were *rated lowest*—the six practices, that is, that many CEO's lacked. These are all soft metrics.

Two of the lowest-rated practices were from the Leading the Organization segment under the category of Leading Change:

- Effectively creates dissatisfaction with the status quo in order to motivate change efforts.
- Effectively influences people who resist change.

Another two were also from the Leading the Organization segment, under the Promoting Innovation and Strategic Thinking, and Making Decisions categories, respectively:

- Facilitates innovation by providing time and opportunity for reflection and brainstorming.
- Effectively delegates appropriate decision-making authority to others.

A single practice from the Leading as a Coach segment under the category of Coaching and Motivating Others was rated the lowest:

- Develops leadership skills of others.

The final behavior in the group of lowest-ranked practices was from the Leading as a Person segment under the category of Openness and Self-awareness:

- Is willing to admit mistakes and change his/her mind.

The first four practices were rated the lowest by two or more of the reporting groups as well as the CEO's themselves. The last two practices (Develops leadership skills of others; Is willing to admit mistakes and change his/her mind) were not seen by the CEO's themselves as a weakness, but two or more of the other survey groups agreed on the low ratings of these practices for their CEO's.

Applying the Integrated Leadership Model

The board can address the lowest-ranked practices (gaps) within the context of the Integrated Leadership Model (ILM; see figure 3.7).

As discussed in chapter 3, the ILM allows boards to assess where the business is on the "S" curve and, from there, to determine what agenda, practices, and leadership style are appropriate for their CEO's. Once the board has determined its organizational needs from its CEO, it should start to think about possible leadership gaps—lowest-ranked practices. My study offered six of the most common leadership practice gaps. The Leadership Compass, as well as other instruments, also gives rating tables that can help the board in its weighting of the practices. The table of Lowest Practice Ratings is the most obvious, but the Practices Relative to Importance Ratings table gives added weight. In an instrument created specifically by the board for its CEO, it would be assumed that all the practices are "important" or "very important" in the assessment of the CEO. In more generic instruments, some practices could be rated as less than important—"somewhat important" or below—and therefore less relevant. In the profile of CEO's that I studied, the lowest-rated practices were all rated as "important" or "very important" to the CEO's success.

Applying the ILM, a board can then examine these practice gaps in the context of its CEO's leadership style. For example, each of the lowest-rated practices identified in my study can be positioned under the four leadership styles:

DRIVER LEADERSHIP

- Effectively creates dissatisfaction with the status quo in order to motivate change efforts.
- Effectively influences people who resist change.

EXPRESSIVE LEADERSHIP

- Facilitates innovation by providing time and opportunity for reflection and brainstorming.

AMIABLE LEADERSHIP

- Effectively delegates appropriate decision-making authority to others.
- Develops leadership skills of others.

ANALYTICAL LEADERSHIP

- Is willing to admit mistakes and change his/her mind.

By combining the ILM with this list of lowest-rated practices, boards can identify the most likely leadership gaps for their CEO's leadership style, and they can discuss these gaps before they become a problem. Furthermore, because CEO's need to modify their leadership style to suit various business cycles, boards can keep these gaps in mind when asking their CEO to shift from one leadership style to another. These six lowest-ranking practices have been put together from my collected group data. Once a CEO has undergone personal assessment, the board can address any other personal leadership gaps as well as these common ones.

So how can the board put this information about potential and actual leadership gaps into practice? Let's assume that the group profile data of CEO's in my study is the individual profile data of your board's CEO and that your business is in a downturn. You need a Driver leadership style from your CEO, but first you need to address the leadership gaps that fall under the Driver style. In a discussion with your CEO, a little tough love coaching might include the following dialogue.

> **Gaps:** Effectively creates dissatisfaction with the status quo in order to motivate change efforts. Effectively influences people who resist change.
>
> *We believe that leadership is the management of change. If you agree, you need to be more cognizant of the importance of managing the downturn our business is experiencing. We understand that it is counterintuitive to "create dissatisfaction with the status quo," but unless our people are dissatisfied with their current state there is little motivation for them to change. We are pleased that you have provided a vision of the future and a path to get there. We know these are critical elements to successful change, but we need you to continually challenge the status quo or we risk not pulling out of this*

downturn. We feel we are at a point that a reinvention of our business must occur to avoid our ultimate collapse.

This exchange begins to confront the practice gaps that surfaced from the CEO assessment. It also includes some information culled from the scholarly literature on leadership competencies, emotional intelligence, and executive derailment. In addition, it draws from the practical experience of this author in conducting leadership development and coaching sessions with hundreds of executives on a global basis. This is one of the reasons that CEO's, with the support of their boards, have professional coaches working with them. Coaches have experience with many different leaders and can help solve a range of problems specific to the CEO.

Now let's assume that the business is no longer in a downturn, but coming out of its trough. Following the ILM, you need an Expressive Leadership style from your CEO. You want your CEO to experiment with new things, but you want to be assured that anything new is thought through before being implemented.

> **Gap:** Facilitates innovation by providing time and opportunity for reflection and brainstorming.
>
> *First, we believe that if we are going to be able to compete against our peers we need to be learning faster than they are. As our CEO, you need to be as effective a learner as you are a leader. You need to be more deliberate in your learning to serve as a role model to others in our organization. You need to take the time to "reflect," to learn from an analysis of our situation and develop alternatives before you "conclude" what our next move should be. We need you to work on that stage of the Learning Cycle. We know there is a greater emphasis in our industry to "plan" and "act" to achieve short-term results, but we feel that this limits the cultivation of our insight and innovation. We need you to maximize our organizational learning. It may be our only truly competitive advantage.*

The Learning Cycle stages referenced in this exchange are based on the work of Honey and Mumford.[6] I first worked with Alan Mumford in 1996, when I was appointed the academic director of Columbia's Executive Education. He collaborated with us to design our methodology for executive learning, which employs the Learning Cycle. The Learning Cycle is based on the finding that "a learning style preference is inferred from the way individuals go about solving problems or behaving in meetings."[7] Thus a manager's ordinary, day-to-day behavior is a great indicator of the way he or she thinks and learns. One of a number of tools used for helping CEO's gain self-awareness of how they learn is Honey and Mumford's Learning Styles Questionnaire.

In addition to bringing in Learning Cycle data, this dialogue confronts the Expressive leader's tendency to learn by doing. Although Expressive leaders can be spontaneous, creative, and willing to experiment, they can also be wrong. The board should try to keep the Expressive leader's intuitive instincts in check by asking for more reflective thinking before action is taken.

In this next scenario, your company is doing fine and your success is growing. Along with this success comes a strong belief about what works for the business. For this success to endure, you need to fortify your leadership bench and have your succession plan fully populated. You need an Amiable leadership style from your CEO, but there are some practice gaps in willingness to delegate and develop others.

> **Gap:** Effectively delegates appropriate decision-making authority to others. Develops leadership skills of others.
>
> *We agree that we have to build a leadership team that will outlive us, in order to assure the company's continued success once we've retired. We need to develop the skills of other leaders, and on-the-job training can't be the only way we accomplish this goal. In that regard, we are concerned that you are not "effectively delegating appropriate decision-making authority to others." We know that this can be difficult because delegating does not remove you from the ultimate responsibility, but it is important for others to be involved in decision-making processes and to develop leadership skills of their own. We want to emphasize that we don't expect nor want you to "do it all." You may prefer to have total control, but we feel that may hinder the development of our next generation of leaders. If you don't "develop leadership skills of others," we will consider it a failure of your leadership.*

In this exchange, the board is confronted with the dilemma of telling its CEO that he or she needs to lead by preparing others to take over—to "build the bench" with a successor. This is a tricky subject, because effective CEO's have a personal need to survive that is just as strong as their desire for their business to survive after they leave. With CEO's that are not Amiable leaders by nature, this can be even more difficult to confront. Edward E. Lawler III, the author of *Talent: Making People Your Competitive Advantage,* asserts that CEO's can be dangerously out of touch with the people they lead, particularly when it comes to the issue of development.[8] Good leaders will address this deficiency. As an example of a positive acknowledgment of this, Lawler points to a statement that Jeff Immelt, GE's chief executive, made in GE's 2005 annual report about what CEO's need to be doing: "Developing and motivating people is the most important part of my job. I spend one-third of my time on people. We invest $1 billion annually in training to make them better. . . . I spend most of my time on the top 600 leaders in the company; this is how you create a culture. These people all get selected and paid by me."[9]

In the last case, the board instinctively knows that business is doing as well as it ever has, but also knows what goes up must come down. The company may be close to reaching a point of inflection, and the board and CEO must manage their risk. Therefore, the board needs an Analytic CEO who will give it the "unvarnished truth" and make accurate assessments and decisions about the future of the company. In this case, your board needs to address the CEO's unwillingness to admit possible mistakes or change its thinking because these factors may make the CEO reluctant to openly discuss risks with the board.

> **Gap:** Is willing to admit mistakes and change his/her mind.
> *We have all been feeling pretty good lately about our performance. All the hard measures—ROA, ROI and ROE—are strong. Our EPS has reached its highest point in our history. You've kept us on a steady path and you've gotten it right. But we want to emphasize that you also need to be clear with us about our risk and be "willing to admit mistakes and change your mind" if you think we're not going in the right direction. We know that this upward trend can't continue forever. We want you to objectively assess our risk, and tell us where we could go wrong. If we can understand this early, we may be able to avoid a total failure in the future. The worst thing we can do is not be totally honest with each other about the state of the business. Now can we talk more about these "derivatives" that we're trading?*

I added that last line because I recently presented a case study on the Lehman collapse to an Outstanding Directors Exchange (ODX) meeting in New York. Richard Fuld, Lehman Brothers' CEO, was an Analytical style leader who didn't like admitting his mistakes, and this leadership gap should have been addressed by his board for his own good and that of the company. Assessing leadership styles and possible gaps, rather than looking only at the hard numbers, can help boards identify problems before they become crippling for the company.

Diagnostics: The Use of Soft Metrics

Today boards have many ways to measure and decide what is required of their CEO's in terms of the hard metrics of the business, but soft metrics, which are not measured as often, allow boards to understand how the CEO got to those hard metrics. Looking at soft metrics gives boards an opportunity to have a dialogue with their CEO's about building long-term strategic value. However, soft metrics are not a one-size-fits-all metric for a CEO. I recommend a more tailored set of hard and soft metrics that assess the agenda, practices, leadership style, and viability of the CEO in the context of where the business is in its life cycle. In other words, choose metrics that will diagnose what is needed for the business (the business cycle), and what's required of the CEO's leadership (agenda, practices, style).

A closer look at the metrics used in determining the performance of Lehman's CEO can help illustrate the importance of both hard and soft metrics. Richard Fuld had been chief executive officer of the company since 1993 and chairman of the board of directors since 1994. In March 2008, the board granted Fuld an award of more than $40 million in cash and stock for, as the proxy put it, "successfully navigating the difficult credit and mortgage market environments and maintaining the firm's strong risk controls." That proxy also commended Fuld for a 104% jump in Lehman's stock price over the prior five years, notwithstanding a 15% drop in fiscal 2007. Fuld, the proxy says, cultivated "an employee-ownership culture that promotes long-term alignment with stockholder interests."[10] In contrast to that proxy statement, Bloomberg, in an article a couple of months after the Lehman collapse, chronicled the following account of the practices of Fuld's leadership style:

An intimidating figure—he played in international squash competitions when he was younger and is still fit—Fuld was known around the office as "the Gorilla." His icy stare, people who worked at Lehman say, froze recipients with fear. No one wanted to tell Fuld something was wrong or to question how Lehman was run. . . .

Management-committee meetings were conducted without discussion, attendees say. The same was true of executive-committee meetings presided over by Fuld. While reviewing budgets for 2007, one committee member questioned the performance of a unit, according to a person who was in the room. Fuld stared at him coldly, then broke the silence: "You've got some balls to say that, knowing how much I hate that topic." As Fuld returned to studying the papers in front of him, Gregory continued dressing down the committee member for his impertinence. He also upbraided him after the meeting, demanding that any objections be brought to Gregory privately and not voiced in front of the committee. Word on proper comportment spread through the ranks. Fuld conducted an employee webcast every three months. He'd always end by asking if there were any questions. There rarely were.

The problem with this authoritarian climate was that when Lehman began to sputter, Fuld was cut off from dissenting opinion. Woe to the messenger who came to the 31st floor bearing bad news. As cut off from information as Fuld may have been, it wasn't as if he didn't recognize the firm's problems. In November 2004, more than two years before the bull market reached its peak, Fuld was telling people around him that low interest rates and cheap credit would create a bubble that could one day pop. "It's paving the road with cheap tar," he told colleagues in a meeting at the time. "When the weather changes, the potholes that were there will be deeper and uglier."[11]

If members of the board had considered these practices or soft metrics, they might have better diagnosed the health of the organization under the Fuld leadership and not provided him with $40 million in cash and stock. Looking back at the practices that make for effective executives, the soft metrics that measure a leader's style as either hierarchical-authoritarian or egalitarian-participatory would have been appropriate. I'll offer more detail about how to make measurements like this in chapter 7, but by way of example, I would have included these leadership metrics in the assessment of Fuld's effectiveness:

- Takes responsibility for communicating.
- Is accessible and approachable for talking about issues or concerns.

- Effectively uses his/her network of relationship inside the organization.
- Thinks and says "we" rather than "I."
- Demonstrates respect for others.

By rewarding Fuld for only the hard metrics of the business, the board was not making a comprehensive assessment of the performance of the business under Fuld's leadership. Sometimes what really matters in the diagnosis of a business is not the numbers but an assessment of the CEO's agenda, practices, and style and its alignment with the needs of the business.

In my 2008 Executive Leadership course, which I teach in the Columbia Business School's Executive MBA program, the Lehman collapse and Fuld's leadership was a hot topic. One of my students had contact with someone still on the inside of Lehman when the dysfunction of Fuld was occurring. The general assessment of Fuld's leadership from this insider was that Fuld had become a captain of the industry by steering the company through more than one near-death experience in the past, and this created a disbelief that Lehman would ever go into bankruptcy on his watch. In the congressional hearing that followed Lehman's collapse, however, Fuld acknowledged the destabilizing factors that began to appear in the last few months of his tenure. These included rumors, widening credit default swap spreads, naked short attacks, credit agency downgrades, a loss of confidence by clients and counterparties, and "strategic buyers sitting on the sidelines, waiting for an assisted deal."[12] Ironically, Fuld was applying not just hard metrics, but soft metrics in the diagnosis of Lehman's collapse.

It is unknown if the Lehman board, Fuld's boss, ever felt a lack of confidence in him. If it did, a little tough love could have gone a long way in leading him to admit his mistakes and change his mind about the way he was doing things around Lehman. This would have been a difficult assignment for the board's Compensation and Benefits Committee, which evaluates the performance of the CEO, since Fuld was also the chairman of the board. However, since Fuld had continued to improve the hard metrics that he was rewarded for by this committee, it's likely that measuring and rewarding the soft metrics could have led to an improvement in those as well. Measurements and rewards should be linked to the needs of the business on the business cycle, including the required agenda, practices, and leadership style of its CEO. If all these factors are being measured and rewarded, the metrics are right for a productive board/CEO partnership. If the board does not apply all these metrics in diagnosing the health of the business and its CEO's performance, as was the case with Lehman and Fuld, a business and its leader can collapse.

In hindsight, it is apparent that Lehman reached a peak on its business cycle but Fuld continued business as usual. He had his way of doing things and wasn't about to change. Although an Analytic style is generally what's needed when the company is at its peak, Fuld's Analytical style was toxic for Lehman because he would not readily admit mistakes or change his mind. Under stress, he shifted to a "tell-assertive" style that left him ill equipped to lead and isolated in the crisis. It took a cataclysmic failure before he considered modifying his style to challenge the status quo and create change in the way things were being done at Lehman. Hard metrics could have diagnosed the poor health of the business but weren't enough to get to the root cause of the illness. According to SeekingAlpha.com, investors should have been asking why Lehman had let its leverage ratio, or total assets divided by stockholders' equity, climb to 30.71 to 1 in the market turmoil of November 2007 from 26.2 to 1 in the peaceful bull market of 2006.[13] But I would add that some of the soft metrics that could have diagnosed the poor health of Fuld's leadership style can be found in Drucker's Practices of Effective Executive practices for "Ensuring the Whole Organization Felt Responsible and Accountable" and Columbia's complementing practices for CEO's (see table 4.1). Specifically, the board could have been assessing whether Fuld *thought and said "we" rather than "I"* and whether he *"demonstrated respect for others."* These intangible assets didn't show up on Lehman's balance sheet, but they definitely showed up in its bankrupt leadership.

The board needs to measure what it wants done and reward what it wants the CEO to continue to do, taking into account both hard *and* soft metrics. When the CEO's leadership practices are directly linked to the organization's needs and subsequently measured and rewarded, the metrics are correctly focused on what really matters in the board/CEO partnership.

5

How the Partnership
Can Go Wrong:
TTWO

Culture: The way we do things around here

Take Two Interactive (TTWO) provides an informative example of a failed partnership between the CEO founder, a 21-year-old genius, and the board. This case was brought to my attention by a fellow business professor at Columbia, David Beim, who developed it and handed it over to me for presentation at a series of Outstanding Directors Exchange (ODX) meetings in New York, Chicago, and San Francisco in 2007. More than just illustrating a failure in the partnership and Social Contract between a board and its CEO, the TTWO case study gives us an opportunity to examine the interdependence of business cycles and leadership agenda, practices, and styles. While presenting this case I will discuss how the Integrated Leadership Model (ILM), if applied with the appropriate level of tough love, could have helped a CEO/board partnership and business from going wrong.

The Gamer Generation

TTWO, a producer of video games for machines like Xbox and PlayStation, was a child of the dot-com era. Founded in 1993 by Ryan Brant, a 21-year-old programmer, the company went public in 1997 and was a hot stock that increased in value through the decade and entered into the new millennium with an impressive set of performance numbers. Brant, a graduate of the University of Pennsylvania's Wharton School of Business, was the CEO of the company from its inception on. This case study will begin looking more closely at the partnership between Brant and his board through the lens of the ILM (figure 3.7).

Leadership in the Beginning and Early Stages

Brant had been the CEO and a director of TTWO since he founded the company. He had two years of prior experience as COO of an illustrated book publisher. The CEO agenda for planning and launching a new business requires responding to a challenge and willingness to experiment. The combination of operating experience and creative ability gave Brant the right leadership practices and style for a start-up company. I have seen students with this Driver/Expressive behavioral profile in the entrepreneurial program at Columbia Graduate Business School, and they are usually action oriented and spontaneously creative with a concomitant need to achieve results and gain approval. Sean Silverthorne sees this type of leadership behavior as particular to the gaming generation:

> Gamers approach the business world a bit more like a game. They see the different companies—and maybe the people they work with—as "players." They're way more competitive and are very passionate about "winning." They are both more optimistic and more determined about solving any kind of problem you can imagine; they think there's always going to be some combination of moves that will result in success. That drives them to be incredibly creative. They're a bit suspicious of company leaders: The game world is not big on following hierarchy. Plus, they are very confident. Like entrepreneurs, they would rather rely on their own abilities to succeed or fail. They're also more comfortable with risks, but aren't reckless.[1]

The CEO looked right for this start-up company. Did the board? Here is the founding board's membership as reported in TTWO's 10K filing.

FOUNDING BOARD

Ryan A. Brant, CEO and director
Mark E. Seremet, president, COO, and director
Thomas Ptak, VP of Creative Development
Barbara A. Ras, controller
James W. Bartolomei Jr, VP Sales
Oliver R. Grace Jr., director
Neil S. Hirsch, director
David P. Clark, director
Kelly Sumner, director

This would appear to be a board that could work in partnership with its under-30 CEO. Seremet and Ptak had both held leadership roles at similar companies, and Ras and Bartolomei had the financial expertise and experience to help the company get started. However, looking more closely at the "independence" of the directors on the board, there are some red flags. Clark was a co-founder of IMSI, a company acquired by TTWO, and Sumner entered into an employment agreement with Take-Two Interactive Software Europe Limited (TTE), a wholly owned subsidiary of TTWO. Because these external directors were primarily investors or vested in TTWO, the focus of the board's partnership with Brant was based on short-term rewards rather than on long-term growth, and on satisfying immediate gratification rather than on sustained health. Brant needed more independent and unencumbered directors to serve as his coaches. This partnership required a Social Contract, a set of operating principles that would ensure TTWO's long-term development. I would prescribe

- *Commitment to values:* a leadership credo that answers the question, "What do we stand for as an organization?"
- *Commitment to the stakeholders:* customers, employees, shareholders, and community.
- *Commitment to risk assessment:* a willingness to manage the company's risk profile.
- *Commitment to transparency:* complete honesty in financial and nonfinancial matters.
- *Commitment to coaching:* for continuous improvement.

Unfortunately, Brant never had a group of directors that could give him honest feedback on his performance, let alone agree on a set of operating principles. In addition, the executive compensation contract with the CEO included a bonus that was dependent on meeting First Call's consensus estimate of EPS each quarter, and the contract with the CFO included a bonus dependent on the company increasing its net income each period.[2] This reliance on these few hard metrics as indicators of success would contribute to the downfall of the TTWO board.

Changes in 1998 and 1999

In addition to the vested interest of the external directors, the board's membership was constantly shifting. The first signs of change on the board become apparent with the first complete 10K published at the end of the 1999 fiscal year. Seremet, Ptak, Bartolomei, and Clark were no longer directors, and Sumner moved up in the batting order to VP of International Operations and director. There was a 50% turnover of external directors, and three new chief administrative officers (CXO's) were added to the board lineup—COO, Anthony Williams; CFO, Larry Muller; and Barbara Ras assumed the role of chief accounting officer (CAO) and secretary. Robert Flug and Robert Alexander joined as new directors.

Despite this constantly shifting board, Brant successfully led his company through its beginning and early growth stages, with a Driver/Expressive style required of the leader, but then TTWO began to move into the middle part of its business cycle. To ensure that the company continued to prosper, Brant needed to shift his leadership style to being more amiable and start enabling others for the business to endure. Instead, he relinquished the CEO role and thus we will never know if he could have modified his leadership agenda, practices, and style. Had Brant continued as CEO of TTWO as it began to move into its more mature stage of development, he and his board would have had to address his leadership capabilities and those of his management team. As it was, Brant remained in his daily operating role, with the title of chairman, and Kelly Sumner took over as CEO in 2000. Looking at the board for the fiscal year ending October 31, 2000, we find very few members from the board at the founding of the company:

Ryan A. Brant, chairman and director
Kelly Summer, CEO and director
Paul Eibeler, president and director
Anthony R. Williams, co-chairman and director
Larry Muller, COO and director
James H. David, CFO and director
Oliver R. Grace Jr., director
Robert Flug, director
Don Leeds, director

During Brant's tenure as CEO, of the four external directors on the board, Grace was the only constant presence. The only thing consistent about the board was an annual turnover in external directors. For Brant to get any constructive feedback, he needed external directors who had seen the company through different stages in the business cycle and who had observed his leadership at each stage. As discussed in the opening chapter, the reinvention of Tyco by Breen and Krol resulted from a strong partnership and a clear set of priorities. This partnership included a board of external directors with the expertise that could guide the company through its new beginning and early rise from the ashes of its previous CEO's failed leadership—a practice that could have served Brant and TTWO well not only during its rise, but at the launch of his start-up.

The First Signs of Trouble

Although the leadership metrics of this company looked troubling, the hard metrics of the business did not immediately indicate this. Financial performance had become the only rule for the success for Brant and his board, and the company's numbers were only getting better. For the fiscal year 2000, TTWO reported a 26.5% net increase in sales and a 53% increase in net income. In the 10K for that year, the board attributed this to "the expansion of our global publishing and distribution businesses, with substantially all of the increase attributable to internal growth." TTWO had acquired numerous small game manufacturers and planned to deliver high-profile game content for both PC and evolving console markets.

This financial success translated into huge compensation packages for Brant and the CFO. Brant's compensation increased 38% in his last year as CEO to just over $1 million, and he was granted 200,000 additional options. As its chairman in 2001, his compensation was increased another 30% and he was granted just under 480,000 additional options.

Right around this time, however, the dot-com bubble burst. Many Internet-based companies that had grown rapidly in the 1990s had not applied standard business models, focusing instead on increasing market share at the expense of the bottom line. By 2001, it became clear that TTWO was having similar difficulties. In February of that year, the company alerted its investors that the Q2 and Q3 earnings would fall short, citing the fact that fewer new games were coming out the pipeline. The year only got worse. In the wake of 9/11, the company had to do a costly reworking of three of its new Xbox games. In addition, Grand Theft Auto, which had been one of TTWO's top games for several years, became the focus of media attention as a contributor to the root causes of violence in the global society. As a result, Australia banned the third version of the game from distribution and the stock fell 31%.

In October, the company's troubles deepened when its accounting methods came into question by the SEC. TTWO was forced to restate the results for fiscal 2000, and the first three quarters of fiscal 2001. Analysts began to suspect that the company had been selling products to itself and then recording those sales as part of its revenues.[3] NASDAQ halted trading in the company's stock in February of 2002 while TTWO dealt with its restatements.

Where was the board in the middle of all this dysfunction? In hindsight, it's clear that the external directors should have asserted themselves at the first signs of accounting irregularities. However, too many of the board members were management cronies, and incompetence was tolerated for too long. Rather than addressing the root problems that led to these accounting troubles—by, for instance, instituting a Social Contract to ensure a commitment to transparency and to the shareholders—the board flushed out some of its old members. Karl Winters replaced the CFO Albert Pastino, and several others joined the board with the priority of overseeing the company's adherence to its operating policies and practices. In 2003, Jeffery Lapin replaced Kelly Sumner as CEO, and Sumner remained on in a developmental role. Although all these changes strengthened the membership of the board and allowed it to address the gaps in the company's leadership and performance, in the end they happened too late to keep the company from becoming dysfunctional.

This dysfunction was not immediately apparent. Even in the midst of TTWO's financial scrutiny, Grand Theft Auto 3 became the top video game in the country for four months, and the stock went up 8% following the announcement of restated earnings. In the first quarter of fiscal year 2002, earnings were reported at $0.82 versus $0.25 the year before.

By mid-2003, earnings were up 58%. The board must have thought it dodged a bullet. However, its reliance purely on hard metrics as indicators of the company's strength and its failure to deal with the dishonesty of its leadership would come back to haunt it.

New York Times Exposé, May 12, 2003

It took the *New York Times* to pull together the story of the root cause of the failed CEO/board partnership and to show that despite intermittent success, something was fundamentally unsound about the company's culture, the "way they did things" around TTWO. The article revealed, for instance, that Ryan Brant's father, who had served prison time for tax evasion, was one of the first major investors in the company and was profiting from the real estate that the company leased from him. In 2001, he came under scrutiny for selling $1.86 million in shares, almost his entire holding, months before the trading halt.[4]

But it wasn't only the family connections in TTWO that aroused suspicion. Both of the CEO's appointed after Bryant came under fire in the article as well. Sumner, for instance, was the president of Gametek before coming to TTWO, a company that sold its British business and other assets to TTWO a few months before bankruptcy in 1997. And Lapin was on the board and audit committee of eUniverse, which was the subject of an SEC investigation after restating two quarters of earnings. This was exactly what Lapin had been hired to clean up at TTWO.

This expose made it clear that the changes in the board in 2001 and 2002 could only serve as a short-term solution. This must have become clear to the company itself as well, because in June 2003 the president, Paul Eibeler, declared that management must focus on accounting irregularities and sales practices. When Brant and Lapin overruled him to press ahead with game development, Eibeler resigned. Nonetheless, the board initiated its own independent investigation of accounting, even though Brant and Lapin insisted that this distracted management from operations. Some members of the board demanded the resignation of Brant and Lapin, whereas others feared a loss of creative talent and management continuity. The company was still successful enough to justify this fear; in October 2003, Grand Theft

Auto San Andreas was released to huge acclaim. Sales for 2003 topped $1 billion, and the stock rose to an all-time high.

However, in December 2003, a SEC Wells Notice reported its plan to file suit against TTWO, Brant, Lapin, and two former officers over accounting practices. The company announced that it would delay filing its 2003 report and restate 5 years of earnings.[5]

Finally, in March 2004, Brant resigned as chairman and director, although he remained as vice president in charge of publishing, a new post. Independent director Richard Roedel became chairman, and when Lapin resigned in April 2004, Roedel took that position too. Paul Eibeler was brought back as president and vowed to clean up accounting. As a result, TTWO reported Q2 earnings that were far below expectations and cut estimates of 2004 sales and earnings. The stock fell to $28.

Shareholder Activism

Although by 2004 and into the 2005 fiscal year the shareholders might have thought the worst was behind them, in July 2005, a hacker published "mod" code for Grand Theft Auto San Andreas that revealed sexually explicit scenes buried in the game. Many retailers took the game off their shelves, and although TTWO stopped producing the game and said it would release a cleaned-up version, Walmart and Best Buy announced that they might not restock the game at all. Sales at TTWO fell by 63% in November 2005, and when the company revised its earnings estimate downward, the stock fell to $19.

In early 2006, numerous new shareholder lawsuits based on a range of charges about business practices, including backdating of management stock options, resulted in an investigation by the board's Audit Committee. The management stalled as the board sought an explanation of the issues, and the chair of the committee resigned, complaining that the board was kept in the dark by management and was not adequately independent. By June 2006, TTWO revealed it had received criminal grand jury subpoenas inquiring into a range of business practices. The stock fell to $10, and the SEC opened an investigation into the option backdating, which Brant plead guilty to in 2007. TTWO announced that five external directors had also received backdated options, including the former Audit chair. These directors agreed to give improper gains back to the company, and TTWO said it would take $42 million in charges relating to backdating.

By March 2007, the TTWO board game was truly over. A consortium of investors holding 46% of the stock announced its intent to oust the board and top management of TTWO, and within a few weeks all but two of the directors were replaced. Upon the close of the 2007 fiscal year, Strauss Zelnick, the new chairman of TTWO, stated:

> Fiscal 2007 was a year of progress for Take-Two, capped by better-than-expected bottom-line financial performance in the fourth quarter. The Company has benefited from initiatives to streamline operations and improve our cost structure, while continuing to expand our portfolio of powerful video game franchises. As a result of this progress, Take-Two today is sharply focused on its core publishing business and is operating more productively and efficiently, while continuing to foster the extraordinary creative talent of our development teams. We are fully committed to building on this solid foundation to produce great entertainment and to enhance shareholder value.[6]

Hindsight: How the ILM Could Have Helped

It's unclear, given the lack of transparency throughout the company, who was gaming whom at TTWO. If there ever was a case where tough love was needed between a CEO and the board, this is it. The root cause of the problem, in part, was that there was not a credible cadre of external directors serving on the board for an extended period of time. In addition, there was no evidence of a Social Contract to guide the company's actions, nor was the board confronting the unethical behavior of its CEO and his management team.

Given these conditions, what TTWO needed as it matured as a company was a CEO whose agenda was to build a management team and culture committed to ethical behavior, to all stakeholders, to risk assessment, to transparency, and to coaching for improved performance. An Amiable leadership style could have helped build productive relationships and institute an ethical way of doing things around TTWO. When the market forces changed, as they always do, the board should have required an Analytical leadership style that could bring greater insight to its strategic thinking and model the way for superior execution of its business plan. Absent this alignment of the agenda, practices, and styles in its CEO with the needs of the business, dysfunction was almost inevitable for TTWO.

The situation at TTWO was unique in that the investor group that spearheaded the revolt controlled nearly half of the company's shares. Also, Brant was the first chief executive to be convicted of backdating stock options. Still, as B. Espen Eckbo, the founding director of the Center for Corporate Governance at the Tuck School of Business at Dartmouth College, says, "The takeover sends a message to directors of other companies that their jobs are in jeopardy if they lose sight of their commitment to shareholders. . . . The pendulum is swinging in the U.S. toward more hiring and firing of directors—the board is being held to a higher standard as we go forward than ever before. Boards are literally being re-educated about what their jobs are."[7]

The leadership failure at TTWO illustrates the need for tough love in the boardroom. Whether TTWO's founder/father combination would have allowed for an open and honest partnership between the board and the CEO is truly suspect, but the lack of any kind of Social Contract or independence from external directors made failure almost inevitable. In the end, it took a revolt from outside to change the executive leadership and the board. David Beim had it right when he said, "The problem is corporate culture. This was a defiant, over-confident, under-experienced crowd with scant regard for social norms or legal niceties. Corporate cultures are incredibly difficult to change once embedded. It was beyond the power of the board to change."[8] Upon further reflection, I would offer that it was beyond the power of this board to change the TTWO culture because it helped create and reinforce it. If the board wanted a different culture, it needed to define its partnership with Brant through a Social Contract that embodied its credo and mandated ethical operating policies and practices. The external directors needed to assert their independence, thereby fulfilling their fiduciary role to the shareholders by diligently monitoring the performance of the CEO. They needed to

Know the CEO's behavioral style and leadership practices.
Know the organization's needs (strategy, priorities, and gaps).
Match the organization's needs with the leadership that is required.
Look first at the CEO and then the senior team to find the correct match.
Look elsewhere if the correct match isn't found.

At TTWO, the board exercised tough love with its CEO too late, rendering it about as effective as not having exercised it at all. This case is a classic example of the tension between a creative genius and sound business practice—complimentary leadership practices and styles that didn't coexist in this boardroom. Boards are loath to lose what makes a creative business special, but they must not forget good management practices in the quest for originality. You can rely on driving independence and a disposition to experiment when starting up a business, but as the business matures there is a need for more enabling leadership and proven business practices.

6

What Directors Need to Know Before Committing to a CEO

Alignment: The levers of the business system working in sync to achieve optimal output.

There are extraordinary circumstances under which it is difficult to conduct an impartial and thorough search for a CEO. At Coke, for instance, the sudden death of Goizueta forced the board to make a hasty decision about the successor, and it chose the Number Two in command without much discussion. At TTWO and JetBlue, on the other hand, the CEO's were also the founders of the companies. These circumstances did not allow for a deliberate approach to the process of committing to a new CEO. However, in ordinary circumstances, there are a few things boards should be sure of before they make any commitment. Most important, directors need to be certain that their choice is a result of congruence between their business strategy, the CEO's leadership, and the levers of their business system.

To help boards make their decision, I have developed a process that is based on my work with two former faculty members of Columbia Business School, Don Hambrick and Mike Tushman. Both men were well-established thinkers in strategy creation and implementation when I began teaching full time in Columbia Executive Education programs in 1996. During my early years, working alongside them with our custom clients, I learned the power of using Hambrick's Strategy Diamond[1] and Tushman's Congruence Approach for managerial problem solving.[2] Both of their processes can be applied to a model that helps answer the crucial question, "What do directors need to know before they commit to their CEO?"

CEO Alignment

I have developed a four-step process for determining if a prospective CEO aligns with the needs of a business:

1. A board needs to fully understand its own strategic context and intent—collectively, its strategy—before it can hope to engage productively in the process of selecting a CEO. Only then can the board move on to the next step:
2. Determine, given the company's position, the agenda, practices, and style required of its CEO.

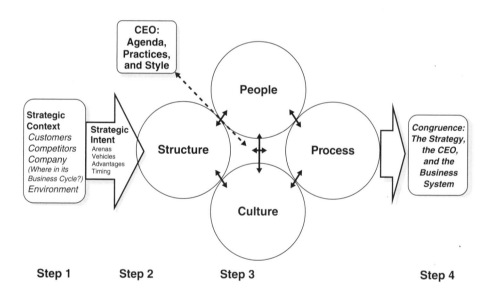

Figure 6.1.
CEO Alignment. (All rights reserved, William Klepper, 2008. Adapted from D. C. Hambrick and J. W. Fredrickson, "Are You Sure You Have a Strategy?" *Academy of Management Executive*, 15, no. 4 (2001); Tushman and O'Reilly, 2002.)

3. The board must assess the alignment of the levers of its business system (structure, process, people, culture) and identify any gaps, because these gaps will become the CEO's strategic priorities. The final step occurs as a result of the first three steps:

4. Achieve a degree of congruence between the strategy, the CEO, and the business system (figure 6.1).

Let's walk through my CEO Alignment Model in greater detail.

Step 1: Strategic Context and Intent

Underlying every strategy is a set of assumptions about the customers, the competitors, the company, and the environment in which the business is operating. For instance, a business might assume that its offerings respond to the hierarchy of needs of its customers, that it is doing things better than its competitors, or that it has a business model that allows it to make money at any particular point in its business cycle. However, the board must continually reassess the business's competitive environment—including its industry, the economy, geopolitical dynamics, and so on—and adjust its assumptions accordingly. A "situation analysis" can help the board understand and reexamine its strategic context. When transitioning to a new CEO, the board must take the time to revisit the assumptions that underlie its strategy by completing this analysis.

Rita McGrath and Willie Pietersen, both of Columbia Executive Education, offer processes for conducting a situation analysis. Again, I've used their methods successfully with clients, most recently with M&T Bank and Ericsson. McGrath's book *Market Busters: 40 Strategic Moves That Drive Exceptional Business Growth*, written with Ian MacMillan, offers "five strategic lenses through which companies can analyze their current business, and includes targeted 'prospecting questions' and corresponding tools to guide executives as they mine areas for growth opportunities."[3] Willie Pietersen, in his *Reinventing Strategy: Using Strategic Learning to Create and Sustain Breakthrough Performance*, emphasizes that "the mission of strategy is to create and sustain an adaptive organization—one that continuously scans and makes sense of its changing environment, learns from its own actions, and modifies its strategies accordingly."[4] His Web site offers even more detail on the questions that should be asked and answered in the situation analysis.[5] Both of these methods can help boards analyze the assumptions underlying their business strategy. If their original assumptions no longer hold, the strategy needs an update before the board can define its criteria for success (the agenda, practices, and style) of its CEO. It is not uncommon for the situation analysis to be outsourced to a consultancy, and in this case it may be appropriate to charge for updating the firm's work and reaffirming or modifying the conclusions it came to. Ideally, the board will be directly involved in the process of updating the strategy, with either its in-house executive team or outside consultancy, so as not to outsource its thinking. A board needs to fully understand its strategy to be able to credibly engage in a strategic discussion with a prospective CEO.

Once the strategic context of a company has been validated, it is time for the board to take a hard look at the strategy itself and determine what might be missing. As referenced earlier, the Hambrick and Fredrickson Strategy Diamond offers a set of elements to help the board in this process. For our purposes, I am focusing on four of the five elements. The fifth element, economic logic, asks, "How will we obtain our returns?" Although the economics of the business is a key factor in determining the viability of the strategy, the board can defer that assessment to the CEO and management team. When the board understands the CEO's concept for achieving the business objectives, it needs to be assured that the plan will result in greater satisfaction of its customers' needs and superior profitability for the business.[6] Eric Abrahamson, a fellow faculty member at Columbia Business School, adapted Hambrick and Fredrickson's Strategy Diamond to include four elements for our work with one of our Executive Education custom clients. We knew that the economies of this client's business were tried and true and felt that the focus on the Arenas, Vehicles, Advantages, and Timing would allow the client to think more strategically. We defined strategy as "the central, integrated, externally oriented concept of how we plan to achieve our objectives," and then presented the four key components of the Strategy Diamond (figure 6.2).

In their article "Are You Sure You Have a Strategy?" Hambrick and Fredrickson used the example of IKEA to illustrate how these four elements can define the strategic intent of the business. Many of these elements can be gleaned from IKEA's mission statement: "IKEA offers a wide range of well-designed, functional home furnishing products at prices so low that as many people as possible can afford them. This is the idea at the heart of everything IKEA does, from product development and purchases to how it sells its products in IKEA stores globally."[7] It is a strategy that is

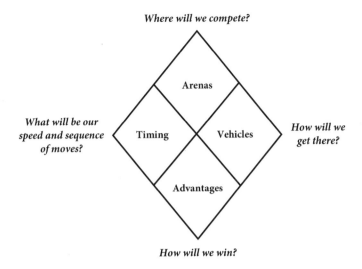

Figure 6.2.
The Strategy Diamond. [Adapted by Abrahamson from D. C. Hambrick and J. W. Fredrickson, "Are You Sure You Have a Strategy?" *Academy of Management Executive*, 15, no. 4 (2001).]

obviously working, as the company's sales were up by 7%, to a total of 21.2 billion euros for the financial year 2008. Hambrick and Fredrickson mapped IKEA's overall strategy using a Strategy Diamond (figure 6.3). (Note: the economic logic of IKEA is found in its economies of scale and efficiencies gained from replication.)

Completing a Strategy Diamond will help the board revise and clarify company strategy and will allow it to determine what it needs from a CEO before it begins speaking with potential candidates. Again, the board shouldn't begin this exercise until it has affirmed its assumptions about its customers, competitors, company, and the environment—the strategic context. If those assumptions have changed, the Strategy Diamond or strategic intent will change as well.

Step 2: CEO's Agenda, Practices, and Style

Let's assume that the board is satisfied that its strategy is based on a reliable set of assumptions and that it is clear in its strategic intent. The next

IKEA

- Inexpensive contemporary furniture
- Young, white-collar customers
- Worldwide

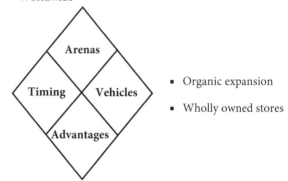

- Rapid international expansion

- Early footholds in each country; fill-in later

- Organic expansion

- Wholly owned stores

- Very reliable quality

- Low price

- Fun, "non threatening" shopping experience

- Instant fulfillment

Figure 6.3.
Ikea's Strategy Diamond. [Adapted by Abrahamson from D. C. Hambrick and J. W. Fredrickson, "Are You Sure You Have a Strategy?" *Academy of Management Executive*, 15, no. 4 (2001).]

step in CEO alignment is to determine where the company is in its business cycle. The board should be able to agree if the business is in a downturn, coming out of its trough, rising, or at a peak. From there it can determine what CEO criteria (agenda, practices, and style) are required to achieve the company's current mission. Again, the CEO Leadership Requirements table can assist in that determination (table 6.1).

Most aspiring CEO's will offer you an assessment of their leadership style if you ask, but you may want to confirm what they tell you by observing their behavior. Short of administering a 360 Social Styles profile, you can look for indicators of their leadership style by watching for Ask/ Tell and Control/Emote behaviors (figure 6.4). In addition, a number of

Table 6.1.
CEO Leadership Requirements

The Business Cycle	CEO Agenda	CEO Practices	CEO Style
Low Success/Beginning Time Frame	Responding to a mandate to change	Challenge the Status Quo	Driver
Rising Success/Early Time Frame	Experimenting; trying new things	Inspire the Future	Expressive
Growing Success/Middle Time Frame	Enduring; doing what works	Enable Others	Amiable
Peak Success/Late Time Frame	Converging on the Status Quo	Model the Way	Analytical

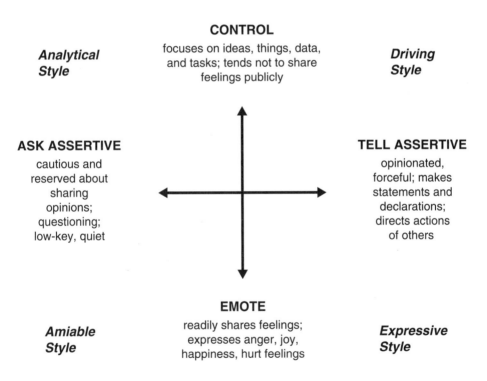

CONTROL
focuses on ideas, things, data, and tasks; tends not to share feelings publicly

Analytical Style

Driving Style

ASK ASSERTIVE
cautious and reserved about sharing opinions; questioning; low-key, quiet

TELL ASSERTIVE
opinionated, forceful; makes statements and declarations; directs actions of others

EMOTE
readily shares feelings; expresses anger, joy, happiness, hurt feelings

Amiable Style

Expressive Style

Figure 6.4.
Leadership Style Indicators. (Source: Improving Personal Effectiveness with Versatility, © The TRACOM Corporation 2007. SOCIAL STYLE and TRACOM are trademarks of the TRACOM Corporation. Visit www.socialstyle.com to learn more.)

Verbal and Nonverbal Cues

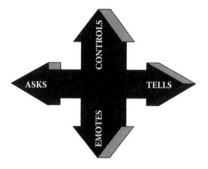

	Verbal and Nonverbal Cues	
Analytical *Style*	1. Monotone 2. Task Subjects 3. Facts/Data 4. Less Hand Movement 5. Rigid Posture 6. Controlled Facial Expressions	*Driving* *Style*

1. Slower Pace
2. Fewer Statements
3. Quieter Volume
4. Nondirective/Relaxed Use of Hands
5. Leans Back
6. Indirect Eye Contact

CONTROLS

ASKS   TELLS

EMOTES

1. Faster Pace
2. More Statements
3. Louder Volume
4. Directive Use of Hands/Points for Emphasis
5. Leans Forward
6. Direct Eye Contact

Amiable *Style*	1. Inflections 2. People Subjects 3. Opinions/Stories 4. More Hand Movement 5. Casual Posture 6. Animated Facial Expressions	*Expressive* *Style*

Figure 6.5.
Behavioral Cues. (Source: Improving Personal Effectiveness with Versatility, © The TRACOM Corporation 2007. SOCIAL STYLE and TRACOM are trademarks of The TRACOM Corporation. Visit www.socialstyle.com to learn more.)

verbal and nonverbal indicators can help determine a leader's style (figure 6.5). However, when using the behavioral charts depicted in figures 6.4 and 6.5, you must be aware that your cultural lens comes with a bias that can cloud your judgment. For example, Ask and Tell behaviors in Japan differ from those in the United States (Japan is more Ask, the U.S. is more Tell). On the Emote and Control dimension, the U.S. norms differ from those in Germany (U.S. more Emote, Germany more Control). I am currently working with an Executive Education custom client based in Mexico and am using a TRACOM Social Style Self-assessment that is weighted for that culture and is written in Spanish. The best guide for observing the behaviors of others is to first take into account their cultural context and to weigh any verbal and nonverbal cues in terms of the norms of that culture, not your own. Ideally, individuals should assess themselves using a self-assessment constructed specifically for their country and culture.

Step 3: The Alignment of the Business System

Every CEO candidate will want to know what is broken in the company and needs fixing. Before speaking with prospective CEO's, the board must determine what is broken—i.e., what levers of the business system are not aligned and, therefore, not supporting the current strategy. This portion of my CEO Alignment Model is again based on the work of Tushman and O'Reilly.[8] These are the levers of the business system as they've defined them:

- Structure
  Definition: The various structures, processes, and systems that are formally created.
  Critical Features: Grouping of functions, structure of units; coordination, control, and linking mechanisms; job and work design; human resource management systems; reward systems; physical location.
- Processes
  Definition: The critical tasks that must be performed in the unit and the associated processes within the unit and between the unit and other areas (both within and outside the firm).
  Critical Features: Degree of uncertainty associated with your unit's critical tasks; nature of work flows within, across, up, and outside the unit.
- People
  Definition: Characteristics of people in your unit and those in interdependent areas.
  Critical Features: Knowledge, skills, and competencies within the unit; individual needs and preferences; background factors; demography.
- Culture
  Definition: The shared pattern of beliefs, assumptions, and expectations currently held by your unit and by interdependent others.

Critical Features: Norms, values; intragroup relations; intergroup relations; informal working arrangements; communication and influence patterns; behaviors and attitudes; power, politics.

All these levers, with their "critical features," are in play when it comes to executing the strategic intent of the company. To continue with the earlier example, figure 6.6 shows the architecture of IKEA and how the company's organizational structure aligns with its strategy.

In Step 3 of the Alignment Model, the board must finish defining its organizational architecture. After mapping out the people, process, culture, and structure that support its strategic intent, the board should ask itself if any of these features are not operable.

For instance, assume for a moment that IKEA's management structure was hierarchical rather than "nonhierarchical" and that sales people were not given the freedom to make decisions without a corporate

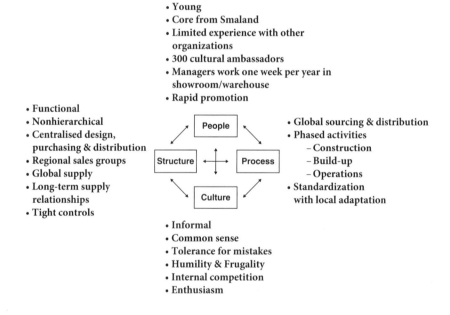

Figure 6.6.
IKEA's Organizational Architecture. [Adapted by Abrahamson from D. C. Hambrick and J. W. Fredrickson, "Are You Sure You Have a Strategy?" *Academy of Management Executive,* 15, no. 4 (2001).]

supervisor approving. For those of you who have had the experience of shopping at IKEA, you'll know that these sales personnel, often young and enthusiastic, are in abundance on the showroom floor. My own experience was with one of their interior designers, whom I talked to about outfitting an entire home that I was building in Colorado. If IKEA imposed a hierarchical structure, this salesperson would probably have had to go to management to oversee such a large purchase. As it was, though, she didn't hesitate for a minute, and during the period of a month, we toured through the showroom and identified all the things we liked, she designed the layout of furnishings and accessories down to the kitchen utensils, packaged them, and had them delivered to the home site—all with free shipping. If I were a member of the IKEA board and were seeking CEO alignment, I would want to be assured that a hierarchical management structure didn't get in the way of that interior designer's youthful enthusiasm for satisfying a customer's request. Wherever structure does not support strategy, the board has a performance gap that should be discussed with the aspiring CEO. These gaps, in turn, become the strategic priorities of the CEO.

Having completed steps 1–3 in the Alignment Model depicted in figure 6.1, the fourth step is for the board to determine the degree of congruence between the board's strategy, the CEO, and the business system.

Step 4: The Congruence Between Strategy, CEO, and Business System

Boards are looking for both strategic leadership and strategic management from their CEO. Strategic leadership, by my definition, requires a specific set of agenda, practices, and behaviors that will result in the "change an organization desires." Strategic management aligns the levers of the business system to achieve that change. Once inserted into the business system, a CEO will serve as either a catalyst or an impediment to a board's desired change. Here are questions the board may want to ask a CEO to determine the degree of congruence:

- *Structure:* How would you align your activities as CEO to achieve the strategic objectives of the business? Does the current design of our organization provide the structure you would need to support our strategic intent? Are there any systems you feel are not aligned?

- *Process:* How would you improve the work flow throughout the organization? What do you feel is the knowledge, skill, and information needed to improve our work processes? Do you feel that our performance measures and indicators are aligned?
- *People:* Do you feel our employees possess the required competencies? Do you envision any changes, and if so, how are they aligned with our employees' expectations and motivations?
- *Culture:* How should we be doing things around here in support of our strategic intent? Are our norms and values aligned with yours, and if so, how?

As the aspiring CEO candidates answer these questions, the board should see if their replies hang together. Does the candidate speak to the connections between the levers and, as a result, describe a balanced and aligned business system? This discussion will be a key indicator of how the individual thinks, and whether his or her ideas are aligned with the board's beliefs. Gaining congruence between your strategy, the CEO, and your business system is a process of discovery whose effectiveness is determined by asking the right questions. Other questions may come to mind, but the ones I've offered are meant to explore all the levers of your business system and their alignment.

Hindsight: The Ewing Township Board of Education

To provide an example of how the CEO Alignment Model could have made a difference, I'll draw from my own experience as a chairman of my home community's board of education. Most of what I'm about to tell you is validated by Bowen's *The Board Book,* but it was not yet published during my tenure on the school board in Ewing Township, NJ.[9] Ewing Township is a suburban school district and is located just north of Trenton. Today Ewing has become an ethically and socially diverse community approaching 40,000 residents.[10] I had been serving on the board of education for two years when I was selected by the members of that board to serve as its president/chairman. During my term as president, the superintendent of eight years retired, and the board began the process of searching for and selecting a new superintendent/CEO.

Looking back, I wish I had crystallized my own thinking about CEO alignment before leading this effort. The board did have a clear definition of its Strategic Context and Intent because the state of New Jersey had laid out what was required to provide a "Thorough and Efficient" (T&E) education—a core curriculum that was comprehensive and a system of free public schools that was cost efficient.[11] In terms of context, the most salient feature was the diversity of the township. Having served as mayor of the township after leaving the school board, I can tell you that we viewed our diversity as a strength that enriched us all. I believe the current mayor of Trenton, Doug Palmer, who had served with me on the Mercer County Board of Freeholders, would agree with me in my assessment that as diverse communities, our school systems were a key contributor to our overall viability. When it came to choosing a superintendent/CEO for Ewing, it was a central criterion that the individual understand and be representative of our socially diverse community.

Today as then, Ewing Public Schools' strategic intent was defined by its mission statement:

> The Ewing Public Schools, an institution governed by the policies, regulations and bylaws developed by the Ewing Public Schools Board of Education and the New Jersey Department of Education, believes that all students can learn. The district's goal is to provide an educational system that dovetails academic excellence with the moral, equal, and respectful treatment of self and others in order to prepare its students to become up-standing, self-sufficient and contributing citizens. This goal will be achieved through teamwork and commitment of the district's network of educators, administrators, board of education members, support staff, parents, elected officials and the greater community. Together they form a partnership whose common vision facilitates, expects and demands ever-improving levels of achievement for Ewing's students and all stakeholders. We will accept nothing less.[12]

In keeping with its mission, the board wanted to "form a partnership" with its new superintendent. This is where the CEO Alignment Model would have been helpful. While the board understood its strategic context (our customers were the students, parents, and community; our competitors were the surrounding school districts; our company was changing its leadership; and our environment was one of limited resources) and had a mission statement that detailed our Strategic Intent, this strategy was not sufficiently defined by a Strategy Diamond, which in hindsight we should have completed. We should have been clear that our Arena consisted of middle-class families whose children were vocationally oriented as much as college-bound. Our Vehicles for delivering a T&E education met standards, but enrichment programs were a luxury. Our Advantages were that we were a fairly homogenous community that supported the cost of a public education for its children as long as they were able to get a job or go on to college after graduation. Finally, we felt our Timing or sequencing of our education—elementary (K–5), middle (6 and 7), junior (8 and 9), senior (10–12)—was working.

Although we missed part of Step 1, we did focus our efforts on Step 2 in the CEO Alignment Model—the Agenda, Practice, and Style required of the superintendent. One of the finalists for the chief executive position was an individual who had served as the acting superintendent of the Princeton School District and was a former elementary principal in its schools. In an effort to learn if her experience matched up with our criteria, another member of the board and I visited Princeton to speak with the network of educators, administrators, board of education members, parents, elected officials, and people in the business community. They all spoke glowingly of her engaging personality and creative spirit as an acting superintendent and principal. Not only was she a strong candidate, but as a black woman she embodied the diversity of the community the superintendent would serve. In 1977, she was selected as the Ewing school district's superintendent by the board and served until 1987. To underline the significance of that choice, the *Journal of Negro Education* in 1982 published a historical overview of the impact of black women in education and concluded that despite racial and gender discrimination, a few highly qualified black women had risen to the ranks of superintendent.[13] Our choice was in those ranks.

Within several years, however, the board began to question the alignment of its CEO with the needs of the community. I left the board after being elected to the Ewing Township Committee in 1980, but observed from a distance the lack of congruence between the superintendent's leadership style and the architecture of the Ewing Public Schools—its structure, process, people, and culture. By way of example, I observed the community's negative response to the closing of a number of the schools in our district. The Ewing School District had maintained the same educational architecture through most of the 1970s, and in 1977, the board had given to its newly appointed superintendent a mandate to change the system. However, we never adequately thought through the gaps she would confront in our existing architecture. In her attempt to address that change, two of the smallest neighborhood elementary schools were closed and a middle school for grades 6 and 7 was eliminated. Her expertise in child development gave her reason to endorse a plan of keeping children in an elementary school environment through the sixth grade and then moving them to a more extended junior high program consisting of grades 7, 8, and 9. Although this move was obviously an attempt to make the kind of change the board was looking for, it did not take into account many other factors in the school system's architecture. As has been attributed to Mark Twain, "It's not change that I object to, it's being changed!" Communities are made up of neighborhoods and their elementary schools were a central part of their identities. In addition, parents felt a certain security when their child's school was within walking distance. The existing architecture (structure and processes) supported the neighborhood culture in the community and people liked it. The new structure and educational processes, even though educationally thorough and efficient, ran counter to the traditional beliefs and behaviors of the parents and children in neighborhoods where elementary schools were closed.

Looking back, it's clear that board oversights in Step 2 of the process—determining the candidate's leadership style—only exacerbated the lack of congruence between the superintendent's leadership and the architecture of the school system. I have fond memories of her 1977 opening of the school year and her address to the faculty and staff of the district, where her Expressive style inspired a hopeful vision of the future for the school district. This style was in keeping with all the laudatory things we'd heard from her former colleagues. However, as her vision for the district was challenged by dissenting views in the community, I could see this Expressive leader become stymied. She began looking elsewhere to satisfy her need for approval, and increased her interest in activities outside of the school district rather than responding to the difficulties she faced on the job.

The board had considered how this candidate performed in "good times," but we were uninformed about her reaction to the "bad times" that were certain to come with our change mandate in Ewing. We did not look closely enough to determine how this individual would perform under the stress of a different set of demands from those she confronted in Princeton. To get a total idea of a candidate's leadership style, the board needs to determine the leadership style of its aspiring CEO both under normal circumstances and under stress. The best way to gain this knowledge is by talking directly to those being led by the CEO as well as others about their impressions of the CEO in both these situations.

I'm sure there are different accounts of how the superintendent's 10-year tenure progressed, but I will always look back with the aid of 20/20 hindsight and believe that the board could have served her and the community much better had it worked more intentionally through Step 2 and Step 3 of the CEO Alignment Model—determine your candidate's leadership style in good times and bad, and assess the organizational architecture to clearly define the gaps. However, this model only existed in the recesses of my mind in those days. And even had we had it, I might have made the same choice. I've since come to realize that I had a personal bias that affected my search and selection of our superintendent/CEO.

The Dangers of Bias and the Power of Persuasion

Directors, in addition to following the four steps of the CEO Alignment Model in their selection process, must be aware of the biases that can influence their choice. I will admit that at the time of our search for a superintendent, I was biased toward an individual who would bring gender and racial diversity to the job in addition to the basic requirements of the position. However, my bias went beyond wanting diversity—I wanted someone like *me*.

As an Expressive leader, my bias was to choose a leader who had the same needs and orientation as I did. My "confirmation" bias, looking for those things that affirm my beliefs, overruled my better judgment. However, this is not an uncommon occurrence in most companies. If you look at the style of individuals who are hired to work in an organization, it is usually the people who are similar to the current leadership that are chosen. Knowing that, I should have stepped back, acknowledged my preference for a leader similar to myself, and reached an understanding with my board on the leadership style that was required if it was change we wanted. According to the Integrated Leadership Model (ILM), that leader would have had predominantly a Driver leadership style. We needed someone who could first challenge the status quo and then inspire the future; first close the gaps, and then experiment with new things—a Jack Welch type of leader. However, I suspect the board and community actually didn't want someone who would challenge and change the way we always did things.

In the courses I've taught most recently, I have gone beyond the confirmation bias to include persuasion science. Robert B. Cialdini's six principles of persuasion are a way to expand on the idea of the confirmation bias:

- *Social Validation:* The first principle is that people are more likely to follow someone who is similar to them than someone who is not. Wise managers, then, enlist peers to help make their cases.
- *Liking:* Second, people are more willing to cooperate with those who are not only like them but who like them as well. So it's worth the time to uncover real similarities and offer genuine praise.
- *Reciprocity:* Third, experiments confirm the intuitive truth that people tend to treat you the way you treat them. It's sound policy to do a favor before seeking one.
- *Commitment and Consistency:* Fourth, individuals are more likely to keep promises they make voluntarily and explicitly. The message for managers here is to get commitments in writing.
- *Authority:* Fifth, studies show that people really do defer to experts. So before they attempt to exert influence, executives should take pains to establish their own expertise and not assume that it's self-evident.
- *Scarcity:* Finally, people want more of a commodity when it's scarce; it follows, then, that exclusive information is more persuasive than widely available data.[14]

These six influencers are clear in themselves, but I'm interested especially in how they come into play when boards are making a decision about their CEO's. I have combined the TRACOM Social Styles and Cialdini principles into a 2-by-2 model in order to provide a clearer understanding of how both can be taken into account for a greater understanding of how personal biases influence decision making (table 6.2). Note that, in my model, the cooperative Amiables and Analytics share the "reciprocity" bias, whereas the competitive nature of Drivers and Expressives makes them biased toward "scarcity" in their decision making.

Let's go back to the case of the Expressive leadership of our superintendent and my leadership style as the board of education president. If you go to the lower-right-hand box of the 2-by-2 model, you'll note that as a fellow Expressive, both of our "Actions Towards Others" were influenced by our support of one another's "Dreams and Intentions" for the school

Table 6.2.
Social Styles and Influencers

Towards Others: Uncommunicative, Cool, Independent

Cooperative, Bias: Reciprocity	*Analytical* Bias: Authority Supports Principles and Thinking	*Driver* Bias: Commitment and Consistency Supports Conclusions and Actions
	Amiable Bias: Liking Supports Feelings and Relationships	*Expressive* Bias: Social Validation Supports Dreams and Intentions

Competitive, Bias: Scarcity

Towards Others: Communicative, Warm, Approachable

Adapted from David W. Merrill and Roger H. Reid, *Personal Styles and Effective Performance* (Boca Raton: CRC, 1981) and R. B. Cialdini, "Harnessing the Science of Persuasion," *Harvard Business Review* (October 1, 2001).

district. This was a good thing in and of itself, but the decision-making bias of Expressives is "Social Validation": they are "more likely to follow someone who is similar . . . than someone who is not." Thus, it is fair to say that I was not the most impartial person to screen this particular candidate. An Expressive will naturally choose an Expressive to work with.

Another factor that I will admit is that I am a competitive person, as are most "tell assertive" people. As my model claims, "tell assertive" Social Styles are influenced by what Cialdini calls "Scarcity." At the time of selecting our superintendent, I knew that she was the only black woman in the country who was considering our superintendent opening, and I wanted our school district to be the first to benefit from the strength of her diversity. When I look back on my interactions with her, she was always communicative, warm, and approachable as those with "emotive" social styles are also known to be. In addition to the factors of Scarcity and Social Validation, she had me at "Hello." Looking back now, I believe that she needed to modify her leadership style to be successful in the job. Being more "ask assertive" would have allowed her first to seek to understand before seeking to be understood. She had offered a clear vision for the future, but her change process needed to include her actively listening to the people directly affected by the change and attending to their natural resistance to change. She needed to be more responsive to feelings and relationships with her detractors if she hoped to be entirely persuasive. However, the change would have been later in coming—if not ultimately given up for lost.

I point out these influence factors not to make the choice of a CEO unnecessarily complex but to make it more unbiased. The lesson for directors is that there is no shortcut to making an informed choice about their CEO. The CEO Alignment Model provides a four-step process to gain greater congruence between the strategy, CEO leadership, and business system. In addition, directors should guard against their own biases in their decision making by being aware of the interplay between their Social Styles and the Six Principles of Persuasion. Having applied these models, directors can better know what they need before they commit to their CEO's. Their due diligence should include investigating the behavior of the prospective CEO in both good and bad times and always being aware of the biases that can cloud a board's judgment.

7

The Board's Commitment to the CEO

Commitment: devotion or dedication (e.g., to a cause, person, or relationship)

Putting Tough Love to Work

Having discussed many things that go into a successful relationship between the board and its CEO, I should reiterate the importance of the Social Contract as the first tool to reach for from the partnership toolbox when building commitment with your CEO. The goal of the Social Contract is to ensure reciprocity in the relationship between the board and the CEO and to foster a partnership that is based on a mutual commitment to a set of behaviors central to their work:

- *Commitment to values:* A leadership credo that answers the question, "What do we stand for as an organization?"
- *Commitment to the stakeholders:* Customers, employees, shareholders, and community.
- *Commitment to risk assessment:* A willingness to manage the company's risk profile.
- *Commitment to transparency:* Complete honesty in financial and nonfinancial matters.
- *Commitment to coaching:* Supporting the CEO and board's continuous improvement.

As I discussed in chapter 1, the board must have an agreement like this in place if it is to fulfill its commitment to the CEO. So what else is needed for the board to be the "best boss" of the CEO? For starters, the partnership between the two must be founded on a common commitment to each other's success. Thus, continuous feedback on how well both parties are meeting their shared commitments is essential to the ongoing health of the board/CEO partnership.

To provide quality feedback to each other, both the board and the CEO must

- Agree on what matters: the metrics of the partnership.
- Take time out at the beginning, midterm, and end of an organization's year to discuss how the partnership is progressing—what's working and what needs work.
- Identify the gaps between the current and desired relationship.
- Set an action plan that will close the gaps and that is measurable and/or verifiable.

Each of these steps offers an opportunity for the board to give its CEO a little tough love, if needed.

Agreeing on Metrics

I discussed leadership metrics in chapter 4. You will recall that there were a series of practices of effective executives based on the work of Drucker and from my work at Columbia Executive Education (see table 4.1).

These are examples of some of the "soft metrics" that boards may want to consider when giving their CEO feedback. Other CEO Leadership Requirements can be added based on what is relevant to the company's business cycle (table 7.1).

Just as a board would confront its CEO for poor performance as measured by the hard metrics of the business, it must contend with its CEO's agenda, practices, and style (the soft metrics) if they are not in alignment with the company's needs. As we learned from the Lehman illustration, this attention to soft metrics can help avoid future problems with the hard metrics. The board can help the CEO and the company succeed by being tough on its CEO about measuring up to these practices and leadership

Table 7.1.
CEO Leadership Requirements

The Business Cycle	CEO Agenda	CEO Practices	CEO Style
Low Success/Beginning Time Frame	Responding to a mandate to change	Challenge the status quo	Driver
Rising Success/Early Time Frame	Experimenting; trying new things	Inspire the Future	Expressive
Growing Success/Middle Time Frame	Enduring; doing what works	Enable Others	Amiable
Peak Success/Late Time Frame	Converging on the status quo	Model the Way	Analytical

requirements. Thus, it's important that the board and CEO *agree on what matters* and decide together what soft metrics they are concerned with. Having an agreement about the metrics of the partnership will allow the board and the CEO to provide each other with productive feedback.

CEO Feedback

A number of pro forma feedback instruments are available that boards can use as a guide for soft metrics. As stated in chapter 4, Ram Charan's *Boards That Deliver* offers an excellent template, but I suggest you tailor the feedback items to what makes sense "here and now" for your business.[1] For example, I would want to incorporate my CEO Leadership Requirements with the practices of Effective Executives. As a result, my CEO Feedback survey would include the items listed in table 7.2.

Having agreed on what's important to measure, each member of the board should complete the feedback form and give it to the chair, or lead director if the CEO is the chair, to compile a summary of the CEO feedback. The CEO should fill out the same form to allow for a self-assessment. To achieve full reciprocity, the board should self-assess its performance on a similar set of criteria and, in turn, receive feedback from its CEO on how it is performing (table 7.3).

Table 7.2.
CEO Feedback

CEO Feedback (circle your rating under each statement or the "?" if you are not sure)

Understands the state of our business
Always   Most of the time   Sometimes   Rarely   Never   ?
Comment:

Has the appropriate agenda for advancing our business
Always   Most of the time   Sometimes   Rarely   Never   ?
Comment:

Exhibits the right leadership practices at the right time to improve our performance
Always   Most of the time   Sometimes   Rarely   Never   ?
Comment:

Employs a leadership style that is congruent with the needs of our organization.
Always   Most of the time   Sometimes   Rarely   Never   ?
Comment:

Check (√) those characteristics that are the strengths of the CEO
A. Gathering Knowledge

( ) Asked, "What needs to be done?"   ( ) Shows enthusiasm for the work we do
( ) Asked, "What is right for the enterprise?"   ( ) Demonstrates s strong personal commitment to high standards of excellence

B. Converting Knowledge into Effective Decisions

( ) Developed action plans.   ( ) Demonstrates perseverance in achieving goals
( ) Took responsibility for decisions.   ( ) Behaves consistently with own words and standards
( ) Took responsibility for communicating.   ( ) Is accessible and approachable for talking about issues or concerns
( ) Were focused on opportunities rather than problems.   ( ) Demonstrates calm and stamina under stressful circumstances

C. Ensuring the Whole Organization felt Responsible and Accountable

( ) Ran productive meetings.   ( ) Effectively uses his/her network of relationships inside the organization

( ) Thought and said "we" rather than "I."   ( ) Demonstrates respect for others

Comment:

Indicate with an (X) the characteristics you feel are weaknesses

Comment:

Table 7.3.
Board Feedback

Board Feedback (circle your rating under each statement or the "?" if you are not sure)

Understands the state of our business

| Always | Most of the time | Sometimes | Rarely | Never | ? |

Comment:

Has the appropriate board agenda for advancing our business

| Always | Most of the time | Sometimes | Rarely | Never | ? |

Comment:

Exhibits the right board practices at the right time to enhance our performance

| Always | Most of the time | Sometimes | Rarely | Never | ? |

Comment:

Employs beliefs and behaviors that are consistent with what we stand for as an organization

| Always | Most of the time | Sometimes | Rarely | Never | ? |

Comment:

What behaviors would you want the board to practice more of to improve the board/CEO partnership?

Comment:

What behaviors would you want the board to practice less of to improve the board/CEO partnership?

Comment

With these tools in hand, the board and CEO should take time out for feedback at the beginning, midterm, and end of an organization's year to discuss how the partnership is progressing—what's working and what needs work. I have facilitated many of these discussions and have learned from that experience how to manage these feedback sessions to make them as productive as possible.

First I have a premeeting with the chair or lead director, as circumstances dictate, to discuss the summary of the feedback for the CEO. I then have a private session with the CEO to review this feedback and prepare him or her for the meeting with the board. In my private meeting with the CEO, I emphasize that feedback should be thought of as a gift, and received in that spirit. I try to make it clear that feedback is not the same as evaluation, and I often use an analogy to explain the difference between them. For instance, "Bill is 6 feet, 3 inches and weighs 200 pounds" is an accurate assessment, whereas "Bill is too tall and too heavy" is an evaluation. If you honestly assess Bill rather than evaluate him, he can accept that feedback as an objective statement about the way others see him. I call feedback a gift because Bill can put this assessment to good use in improving his practices—maintain a Body Mass Index of less than 25!

With that prepping done, I ask the CEO to look at her or his self-assessment and compare it with the summary response from the board members. I have them pay particular attention to the comment section, as this always provides a fuller meaning to what is presented in the ratings.

This premeeting is meant to prepare the CEO for the meeting with the board and to begin to identify the gaps between their current and desired relationship. A checklist for getting the CEO ready includes the following:

- Identifying gaps in perception and looking for themes like
  –Strengths you don't see in yourself but the board does.
  –Areas for improvement that you weren't aware of.
  –Confirmation and/or disagreement with your perceptions.
- Identifying major themes and the "story" of your feedback—what your feedback says about your understanding of the state of the business, your leadership agenda, practices, and style, as well as your executive effectiveness.
- Managing your reactions and planning how you want to respond to the people who gave you feedback.

The board can prepare for the meeting by using a similar checklist to review the CEO's feedback for them. It is assumed that the board members have completed a self-assessment using the same feedback instrument. The chair, or lead director where appropriate, should compile the individual self-assessments into a group composite, and go on to

- Identify gaps in perception, look for themes, such as
  –Strengths you don't see in the board but the CEO does.
  –Areas for improvement that the board wasn't aware of.
  –Confirmation and/or disagreement with the board's perceptions.
- Identify major themes and the "story" of the CEO's feedback—behaviors the board needs to practice more of or less of to improve the board/CEO partnership.

- Manage its reactions and plan how the board wants to respond to the CEO feedback.

Identifying the Gaps

Once the board and CEO have completed their individual preparation, they are ready to meet together. Outside facilitators are not necessary, although they can help oversee the process while the board and CEO focus on their task of identifying the gaps between the current and desired relationship. A basic gap analysis requires the board and CEO to

1. Clearly define expectations and goals—vision for the board partnership.
2. Document the gap (i.e., the differences between expected and actual practices and behaviors).
3. Prioritize the gaps.

Where can the board and CEO start the discussion of their expectations and goals? When I facilitate these meetings, I advise them to begin where I began this book—by looking at the Social Contract, where the vision for their board partnership is embodied. By considering a statement of what the board stands for alongside an assessment of each other's practices and behaviors, the board and the CEO can better understand and prioritize any gaps.

A root-cause analysis is the best way to understand and document the differences between expected and actual practices and behaviors. Such an analysis starts with the question, "What are the fundamental, systemic causes of current gap?" I encourage the board and CEO to ask themselves this question at least three times, so as not to prematurely accept a symptom of the gap for its root cause. To facilitate this process I have them map out these symptoms as causes, as shown in the "Why-why" diagram (figure 7.1). I then ask them to step back and synthesize their analysis to ensure that the diagnosis is comprehensive and has addressed the partnership in its totality—its structure, process, people and culture. The final task is to rank the list of root causes by importance.

For example, let's assume that the board has taken my advice and listed, as part of its Social Contract, a commitment to coaching for continuous improvement: "We believe in the continuous development of the board/CEO skills and abilities and, therefore, commit the time and resources to learn how we can better perform in our respective roles. We view this as an obligation to our stakeholders and an investment in our future success."

Let's further assume that the feedback from the CEO to the board is as follows:

Exhibits the right board practices at the right time to enhance our performance

Always   Most of the time   Sometimes   Rarely   Never   ?

Comment: **I am not always confident that our directors are keeping up-to-date on the best practices of outstanding boards.**

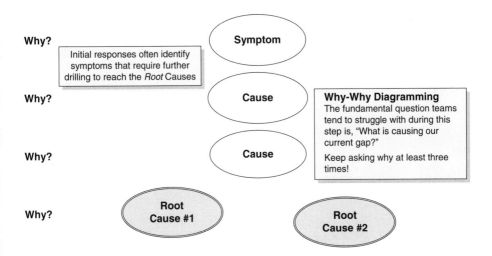

Figure 7.1.
Why-Why Diagramming. (Source: Eric Abrahamson.)

The root-cause analysis of this gap can be found in a Why-Why diagram. I give full credit to Eric Abrahamson for the logic and design of the diagram in figure 7.1.

If you brainstorm and complete the diagram for the feedback given in figure 7.1, you may get a chart that looks like that in figure 7.2.

With these root causes identified, it's possible for the board to set an action plan that is measurable and/or verifiable and that will close the gaps. The third "why" usually uncovers the way to closing the gap (e.g., share best practices learned from serving on other boards that can enhance this board's performance; attend ODX meetings and discuss the key insights gained with the board at our next meeting).

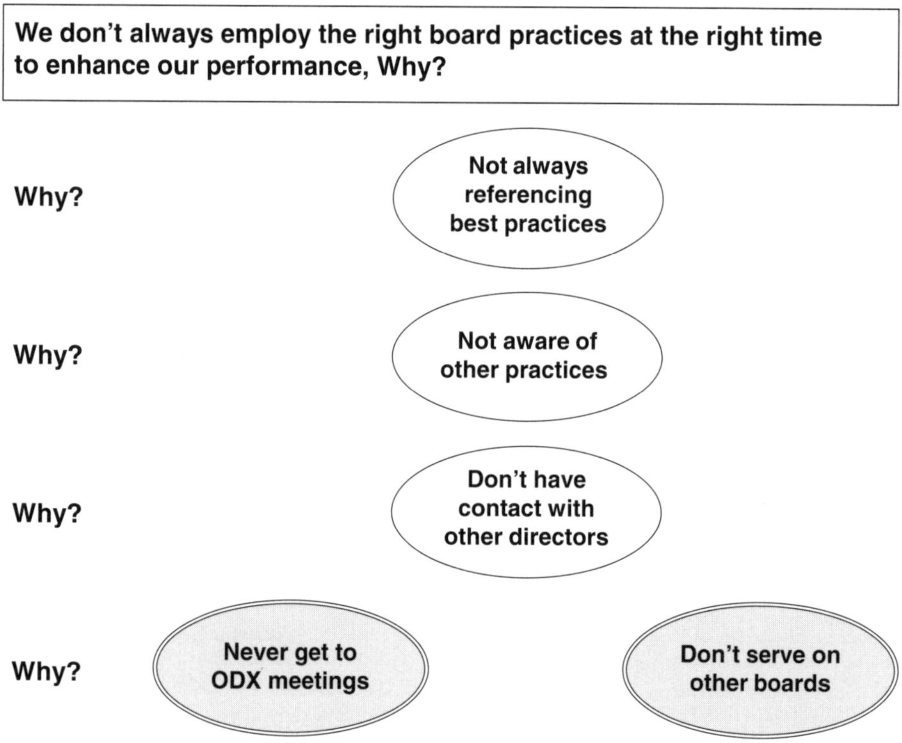

We don't always employ the right board practices at the right time to enhance our performance, Why?

Why?   (Not always referencing best practices)

Why?   (Not aware of other practices)

Why?   (Don't have contact with other directors)

Why?   (Never get to ODX meetings)   (Don't serve on other boards)

Figure 7.2.
Why-Why Diagramming in Practice.

Solutions and Action Plans

Again, what "gets measured, gets done" when it comes to improving the board/CEO partnership. However, many CEO's improvements can be measured only in soft, not hard, metrics. Changes in behavior can be easily observed and verified, but they cannot be easily quantified. This is why I encourage boards to look at their feedback at three points in the year— the beginning, the midterm, and the end. At each period, the board can verify what, if any, movement there has been in its assessments. Let's assume we have feedback to the CEO from the board at these three periods and it appears as shown in the following:

Beginning

Understands the state of our business

Always   Most of the time   Sometimes   Rarely   Never   ?

Comment: **We are fortunate to have a CEO who understands our business so well.**

Mid-term

Understands the state of our business

Always   **Most of the time**   Sometimes   Rarely   Never   ?

Comment: **We continue to feel good about our CEO's understanding, but are concerned about the crisis in the financial industry.**

End

Understands the state of our business

Always   Most of the time   **Sometimes**   Rarely   Never   ?

Comment: **We feel we do not fully understand the impact the crisis in the financial industry is having on our risk profile.**

If this was the composite assessment of the CEO's understanding of the state of the business from the start through the end of a year, you have verified that "understanding" has deteriorated in the eyes of the board. This information doesn't provide a hard metric on the performance of the business, but it does help the board identify a clear gap that needs to be closed. Again, the comment section may provide insight about the root cause of the widening gap in understanding. In this case, the board and CEO could have addressed, at the midterm, the decline in understanding from the beginning of the year. If, at the end of the year, there is an assessment of further decline in the CEO's "understanding," there is even a larger gap to close. Again, all this feedback is based on soft metrics but is still significant information that can help improve the quality of the board/ CEO partnership. If the comment from the board can be drilled down, as in the Why-Why Diagram in figure 7.3, to the root cause of the board's feelings, a solution can be identified and an action plan put in place.

In solution building, the board and CEO are looking to identify what specific, concrete action can be taken to address each of the fundamental root causes of the gap. Brain-storming is a well-established process for generating solutions by teams and can be applied here. The team is asked to envision how the board/CEO partnership would have to change in order to eliminate the CEO's understanding gap(s). It suspends all judgment in the initial parts of the process and instead pushes for innovative solutions. In addition, to ensure that solutions are comprehensive, it generates solutions to address the root causes wherever they fall—structure, process, people, and culture.

Possible solutions that could be generated from this root-cause analysis might include the following:

1. A fuller description of our risk architecture.
2. A clearer understanding of our risk management process.
3. An ongoing identification of current and new risks.
4. A definition of the roles and responsibilities of those responsible for risk management.
5. Plans for rewards and recognition of risk management.
6. A timely appraisal of risk for the board.

Once the board/CEO has articulated its solutions for closing the gaps, it can move on to action planning. The brain-storming process will yield a number of possible solutions, so the board/CEO will need to evaluate the

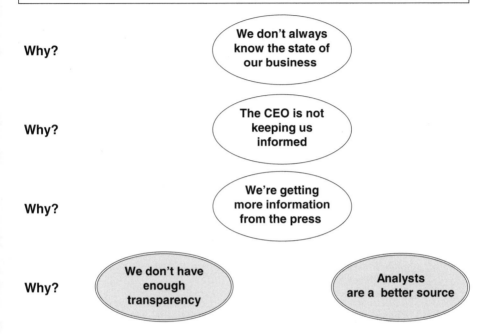

Figure 7.3.
Why-Why Diagramming in Practice, Part II.

solutions and select key actions for each root cause—those essential few
that will make the biggest difference. Having culled the solutions, the
standard Action Planning steps follow:

1. Identify the individuals or groups who will be responsible for
   implementation.
2. Establish realistic but challenging deadlines.
3. Identify what resources are available and what will be needed.
4. Recognize and deal with the barriers to the plan.
5. Determine how progress will be measured and reported.

So what might a completed board/CEO Action Plan look like? Here I
am using the Institute of Internal Auditors Research Foundation as a

Table 7.4.
Quick Hits

	Easy	Difficult
Small Payoff	**Quick Hits**	Caution— Defer
Big Payoff	Gems	Extra Effort— Rework

Table 7.5.
Board/CEO Action Plan

Key Issue: Board/CEO "always" understands the state of the business

Reccommended Action: Monthly briefing of the board by the CEO on the Risk Profile of our business in light of the current economic downturn

Detail actions and milestones	Responsibilties	Timing
1. Effective risk architecture	Management	1Q
2. Risk management process	Risk Officer	1Q
3. Identify current and new risks	CEO	ASAP
4. Roles and responsibilities defined	Management	1Q
5. Rewards and recognition of risk management	Management	3Q
6. Timely appraisal of risk	Risk Officer	ASAP

Metrics: Beginning, midterm, and final feedback—"always" understands the state of the business; risk architecture covers all risk categories; all significant risks being managed

Barriers and Strategies to Overcome Barriers: Shared conceptual definition of risk with common terminology—operations, financial reporting and compliance communicating clearly daily

Resources Available: CEO, Management, Risk Officer

Andditional Resources Needed: Reports from industry and financial analysts; board expertise

source to populate the detail actions and going for a "Quick Hit"—those actions, depicted in table 7.4, that are easy to do and provide immediate, albeit small, payoffs.[2]

The Action Plan format has evolved from my work with our Executive Education custom clients, again drawing from the logic and design talents of Eric Abrahamson, Mike Fenlon, Rita McGrath, and others. This is a sample plan for ensuring that the board/CEO understand the state of the business.

The information itemized in table 7.5 is the output from a process dedicated to the ongoing health of the board/CEO partnership. It is tough love because it is based on open and honest feedback. At the same time, it allows the board to assert its role as the CEO's boss, empowering both its independence and enhancing its fiduciary role—clearly being called for of late by the SEC and company stakeholders. The board's use of "tough love in the boardroom" shows a true commitment to the CEO and organization functioning over the long run.

8

Effective Board Dynamics:
How Directors Interact as a Team

Effective teams have members with complementary
skills and can generate synergy through a coordinated
effort which allows each member to maximize strengths
and minimize weaknesses.

The group dynamics of the board depend on the stage of the board's development, the mix of its members' styles, and the leadership behavior and roles directors employ. Effective board dynamics optimize the conditions for a successful partnership between external and internal directors in the boardroom.

Team Stages and Team Roles

Bruce Tuckman's model explains that as the team develops maturity and ability, relationships are established between members and the leader changes leadership style.[1]

Forming. High dependence on leader for guidance and direction. Little agreement on team aims other than those received from leader.

Storming. Decisions don't come easily within group. Team members vie for position as they attempt to establish themselves in relation to other team members and the leader, who might receive challenges from team members.

Norming. Agreement and consensus form among team members, who respond well to facilitation by leader. Roles and responsibilities are clear and accepted.

Performing. The team is more strategically aware; the team knows clearly why it is doing what it is doing. The team has a shared vision and is able to stand on its own feet with no interference or participation from the leader.

Certain roles become important at different stages of the team's development. Cardona and Wilkinson of IESE Business School originally introduced the alignment of roles and stages in 2006.[2] They raised the question, "How can team members' aptitudes be used to assist the team at its various phases?" A translation of that thinking is depicted in figure 8.1.

Meredith Belbin studied teamwork for many years and observed that people in teams tend to assume different "team roles." He defines *team role*

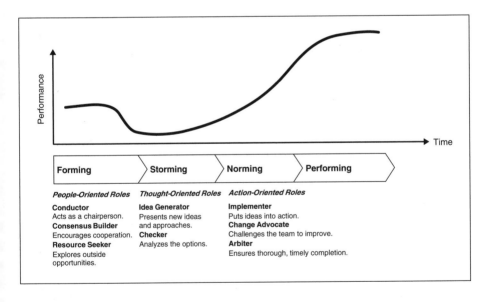

Figure 8.1.
Roles and Phases of Teamwork. (W. M. Klepper, 2009. Adapted from Bruce Tuckman, "Developmental Sequence in Small Groups," *Psychological Bulletin* 63 (1965): 384–99; Pablo Cardona and Helen Wilkinson, "Team Work," IESE Business School, University of Navarra, Occasional Paper no. 07/10-E [December 2006].)

as "a tendency to behave, contribute and interrelate with others in a particular way," and he named nine such team roles that underlie team success.[3] Belbin's team roles are based on observed behavior and interpersonal styles.

PEOPLE-ORIENTED ROLES

- **Conductor.** Acts as a chairperson.
- **Consensus Builder.** Encourages cooperation.
- **Resource Seeker.** Explores outside opportunities.

THOUGHT-ORIENTED ROLES

- **Idea Generator.** Presents new ideas and approaches.
- **Checker.** Analyzes the options.

ACTION-ORIENTED ROLES

- **Implementer.** Puts ideas into action.
- **Change Advocate.** Challenges the team to improve.
- **Arbiter.** Ensures thorough, timely completion.

Boards can better manage their dynamics if they make an objective assessment of their phase of development and use the strengths of their members to leverage them in their teamwork. Absent this information, the ability of the board to generate synergy is severely limited.

Failure of Tough Love: The Learning Studio

My first board experience in business was with The Learning Studio (TLS). This adult education company was established in 1996 and was taken from concept to reality by its founder and CEO—an entrepreneurial, Expressive leader. I joined the board in 1998 as one of its external directors, as the company was expanding its facilities from one to four locations in New Jersey and Pennsylvania. It was during the dot-com boom that this business created a Web site to expand its offerings through the Internet. Initially, the Internet was the channel of 11% of the company's revenue. It was hoped to position the company as the first "Click and Mortar Company" in the industry. The CEO had responsibility for all marketing, operations, and human resources issues; had readied the company for franchising; and raised funds totaling $1.8 million from private investors. However, before the first franchise had been sold, TLS filed for Chapter 7 in the spring of 2001. What are the lessons I learned about the board dynamics during the rise-to-fall in the business of TLS during my tenure as a director?

As was the case with JetBlue, our charismatic, entrepreneurial leader provided guidance and direction during the initial formation of the board. In my case, as with many charter directors of start-ups, entry to the board came about by way of a personal solicitation from the founder—notwithstanding a solicitation of capital. Nonetheless, once the board is fully constituted, the dynamics change—it's no longer personal. Ideally, each member of the board brings a unique set of skills that can be utilized to advance the business. In the case of TLS, we were just beginning to get to know one another's strengths when the weaknesses of the business became apparent. Our CEO was expanding the business more than its capital could support. The initial business plan for community-based adult learning centers was working, but the venture into the internet was eating cash and ultimately created insolvency. So where was our board?

We had moved from our initial formation in which we were dependent on our founding CEO for guidance and direction to a "storming" stage in the TLS board's development as a team. I facilitated a workshop with management and board members to clarify and confirm our winning strategy—what we did better than or different from our competition that created greater value for our customers and superior profits for us (in keeping with the Pietersen prescription). We reaffirmed that the "bricks" or studios were what satisfied the higher needs of our customers and that the "clicks" or internet on-line classes were simply an extension of our product offering. Nonetheless, there had been an investment in the "clicks" side of our business that was creating a cash flow crisis. I reported to the board that Columbia Business School had joined in a partnership, along with a number of other top-tier schools, with a comparable "clicks" venture to which we would provide the intellectual capital for a series of on-line classes. Having just returned from that company's corporate site, I informed our board that its burn rate was in the neighborhood of $1 million/

day. This gave me reason to question why TLS was heading down this "clicks" road—a road to ruin.

Looking back, the TLS board should have applied some tough love and confronted its CEO about this unsustainable "clicks" as an extension of our business offerings. The board never reached a stage in its development where it could come to an agreement on where the business should focus its limited resources, because at this point the business was cash poor. Had our board reached a consensus on our strategy in good times, we would have had a better chance of maximizing our strengths, minimizing our weaknesses, and creating a productive partnership with our CEO.

Formula for Success

When working with teams within various companies, I start with a formula for success (adapted from Merrill and Reid's work):

- Know Yourself
- Control Yourself
- Know Others
- Do Something for Others

I typically present this on a PowerPoint slide, with each element of the formula building on what precedes it. When I finish explaining "Know Others," I indicate that the final element logically flows from the previous and ask them to tell me what it is. Invariably, someone will shout out, "Control Others!" After I commend the speaker for his or her honesty, I emphasize that successful teams work more effectively using a participatory rather than an authoritarian approach, so "Controlling Others" is not a preferred option. On the other hand, "Doing Something for Others," which is what I was asking for, builds social capital and reciprocity in a group and serves to build teamwork. This formula for success is supported by the writings on emotional and social intelligence that Daniel Goleman published in 1996 and 2006.[4] Goleman defines Emotional Intelligence (EQ) as one's "self-awareness and self-regulation"—Know Yourself and Control Yourself. In addition, he defines Social Intelligence (SI) as a person's empathy and social skills—Know Others and Do Something for Others. As a result, EQ and SI defines one's competence, both personally and interpersonally (table 8.1).

Table 8.1.
EQ and SI in Teams

Emotional Intelligence	Social Intelligence
Personal Competence	Interpersonal Competence
"Yourself"	"Others"
Self-awareness	Empathy
Self-regulation	Social skills

Adapted from Daniel Goleman, *Working with Emotional Intelligence* (New York: Bantam Books, 2000).

Know Yourself

The Ancient Greek aphorism "Know Thyself" got it right. Board members can't expect to work effectively with other members and their management unless they can understand how they interact with others. In chapter 3 I presented the Social Styles model as a good starting point for understanding the behavioral style and leadership practices of your CEO. It's also a good tool for board members' self-assessment and can help members better understand themselves and build their self-awareness.

You will recall that there are four major Social Style types, and individuals usually have a combination of a primary and secondary style. Effective board members need to know about their style behavior and how others relate to them. Merrill and Reid offered a set of suggestions based on their original research of human interactions that can allow board members to improve their relationships with others (table 8.2).

By being aware of how their leadership behavior is perceived by others, individual board members will be better able to move to the next element of the team success formula—Control Yourself.

Control Yourself

Once you have a good bead on your behavioral style and how others relate to it, the next step is to control the behaviors that others find

Table 8.2.
Know Yourself—As Others See You

Driver Style

Other Drivers	They see you as action oriented, in a hurry, bossy, commanding, efficient, stubborn, disciplined, tough, independent, secretive, logical, demanding, nonlistening, quick, decisive, unfeeling.
Expressives	Relate to your accomplishments, independence, decisiveness.
Amiables	Relate to your efficiency and discipline.
Analytics	Relate to your efficiency, logic, command of data, and task orientation.

Expressive Style

Other Expressives	They see you as outgoing, enthusiastic, warm, opinionated, talkative, intuitive, emotional, stimulating, imaginative, impulsive, excitable, loud, flashy, dramatic, personable, competitive, caring.
Drivers	Relate to your outgoing, imaginative, competitive and personable aspects.
Amiables	Relate to your warmth, enthusiasm, and your stimulating and personable nature.
Analyticals	Relate to your imaginative, stimulating, thought-provoking nature.

Amiable Style

Other Amiables	They see you as supportive, quiet, friendly, shy, retiring, team oriented, helpful, kind, thoughtful, slow to act, nonthreatening, soft-hearted, easy-going, complying, responsive, open, willing, careful, cooperative.
Drivers	Relate to your supportive, helpful, team-oriented, careful nature.
Expressives	Relate to your supportive, friendly, responsive, helpful characteristics.
Analyticals	Relate to your cooperative, careful, quiet, thoughtful and willing ways.

Analytics

Other Analyticals	They see you as thoughtful, wanting more facts, conservative, quiet, critical, logical, cool toward others, thorough, cooperative, distant, reserved, stern, austere, dependable, accurate.
Drivers	Relate to your logic, command of data, accuracy, dependability.
Expressives	Relate to your cooperativeness, dependability.
Amiables	Relate to your cooperative, conservative nature, accuracy, patience.

EFFECTIVE BOARD DYNAMICS   109

Table 8.3.
Control Yourself—What Others Question

Driver Style

Expressives	Question your coldness, lack of playfulness, critical nature, discipline.
Amiables	Question your lack of feeling, tough-mindedness, bottom-line orientation, impatience, secretiveness.
Analytics	Question your haste, bossiness, decisiveness, competitiveness, risk-taking.

Expressive Style

Drivers	Question your rah-rah, demonstrative, impulsive, emotional side.
Amiables	Question your outgoing, loud, dramatic, impulsive side.
Analyticals	Question your ability to perform as stated, follow-through, and loud, flashy, emotional side.

Amiable Style

Drivers	Question your lack of initiative, need for detail, small thinking, responsive side.
Expressives	Question your slowness to act, and careful, complying, noncompetitive stance.
Analyticals	Question your soft-hearted, easy-going nature, emotional responses, and compliance with others.

Analytics

Drivers	Question your overabundance of facts, lack of decisiveness, and lack of risk-taking
Expressives	Question your dependence on facts, critical, stuffy nature, impersonal approach, lack of fun
Amiables	Question your lack of warmth and close relationships, dependence on figures

Reprinted with permission from Improving Personal Effectiveness with Versatility, © The TRACOM Corporation 2007. SOCIAL STYLE and TRACOM are trademarks of The TRACOM Corporation. Visit www.socialstyle.com to learn more.

abrasive. First, we can assume that a like-styled person will "know one when they see one" and will be more understanding and accepting of your behavior. However, anything in excess will eventually wear thin with people with like styles. Let's focus, then, on what other people in the boardroom may question about your behavior. Consider the information in table 8.3, from the original work of Merrill and Reid. You can see from the table that the key is not only to know yourself but to be able to control yourself. However, you can't stop having developed just your emotional intelligence and personal competence if you want to achieve effective team dynamics on the board. You need to move your perspective from yourself to others—engaging your social intelligence and interpersonal competence.

Know Others

My work with boards always includes a 360 Social Style Assessment of each member by others on the board. I ask board members to consider this feedback along with their own self-assessment and then place themselves on a Social Style fourfold chart in front of the group. This will give the board an immediate, visual idea of what types of leaders compose their group.

By knowing each other's social styles, board members can be more empathetic about the need and orientation of others. This can make the teamwork on the board more harmonious and productive and will allow the members to be more intentional in their efforts to "do something for others" (table 8.4).

Table 8.4.
Know Others

Style	Need	Orientation
Driving	Results	Action
Expressive	Approval	Spontaneity
Amiable	Security	Relationships
Analytical	To be right	Thinking

Reprinted with permission from Improving Personal Effectiveness with Versatility, © The TRACOM Corporation, 2007. SOCIAL STYLE and TRACOM are trademarks of The TRACOM Corporation. Visit www.socialstyle.com to learn more.

Do Something for Others

As I've said, you cannot hope to succeed as a member of a board team by controlling others. On the contrary, worth on a team is built from "what you do for others," and eventually you build up enough social capital that you can begin to spend it. You'll recall that one of the powerful persuaders is reciprocity—do a favor before seeking one. Teamwork is much like a joint savings account into which all members contribute something, and then live off the interest. It's easier to be helpful to others if you have an idea of how they do things and like to see things done. Thus, taking social styles into account is a good way to determine how you can "do something for others." The suggestions of Merrill and Reid for knowing your own Social Style show how you can increase your value to other board members by considering their style needs and orientation (see table 8.5). You will notice that with "fellow" styles in the boardroom, you can't get away with doing what works for you just because these directors understand and accept your need and orientation. In fact, when working with a board in which your social style dominates, you need to be even more aware of your weaknesses—too much of the same role behavior is a limiting factor in the team's development.

Requirements for Teamwork

You may have noticed that there are some striking similarities between "The Roles and Phases of Teamwork" diagram (see figure 8.1) and my ILM. This is no coincidence. The board and its chairperson/leader have as many requirements in developing teamwork in the boardroom as the CEO has in developing the overall business (table 8.6).

The "Behavior" is from the work of Hersey and Blanchard and their Situational Leadership model:

- *Directing:* The chairperson defines the roles and tasks of the members, provides strong direction, and monitors contributions closely. Decisions are made by the chairperson, with little or no feedback from members.
- *Coaching:* The chairperson still defines roles and tasks but also asks for feedback and suggestions from the members. The chairperson is still the decision maker, but there is more communication between the chairperson and members.

Table 8.5.
Do Something for Others

Drivers
For Fellow Drivers: Like you, getting results is important to this person
–Help this person to take the time to listen carefully to another's input
–Allow this person to get things done without unnecessary distractions
–Make sure you share the same goals to avoid finding yourselves charging in opposite directions
–Complement this person's need to tell by asking questions

For Expressives: Remember that personal approval and recognition are important to this person
–Allow for some fun and spontaneity from this person
–Encourage this person to think more about facts and details and to validate and substantiate his or her ideas
–Allow this person to discuss his or her feelings and opinions
–Listen openly to his or her input

For Amiables: Remember that personal security is important to this co-worker and that the relationship with you could be just as important to this person as the task
–Encourage this person to focus on the goal
–Slow down your pace
–Allow for some level of informality in the interaction
–Allow this person to share his or her feeling

For Analyticals: Remember that details and getting it right are important to this person
–Allow this person time to think things through
–Take time to listen carefully and patiently to the details (even if it's more than you want to know)
–Slow down your pace
–Offer direction to help this person make decisions or draw conclusions
–Follow through on your commitments

Expressives
For Fellow Expressives: Like you, personal approval and recognition are important to this person
–Be careful not to compete
–Encourage fact-finding to support ideas
–In addition to focusing on the big picture, focus on necessary details

For Drivers: Be task-oriented with this person
–De-emphasize feelings
–Be organized in your communication
–Avoid power struggles
–Use less small talk, get to the point
–Avoid overgeneralizing
–Provide options and let this person decide the best course to get things done

For Amiables: Listen to this person more often and listen with empathy
–Open with some small talk
–Slow down your pace
–Decrease your intensity
–Don't interrupt
–Be supportive
–Acknowledge importance of relationships

For Analyticals: Slow down your pace with this person
–Listen more often and more accurately
–Pay attention to the details
–Don't come on too strong
–Be task-oriented and systematic
–Take time to be patient with this person
–Give this person time to "think about it" before making a decision
–Follow through on your commitments

(continued)

Table 8.5. (*continued*)

Amiables

For Fellow Amiables: Like you, personal security and relationships are important to this person
–Be careful not to overcompromise or overaccommodate
–Be sure that you use your time together efficiently
–Don't lose track of time in casual conversation
–Acknowledge his or her relationship with you

For Drivers: Pick up the pace when working with this co-worker
–Demonstrate high efficiency
–Be task-oriented
–De-emphasize feelings
–Be clear about goals and plans
–Use less small talk and get to the point
–Be organized in your communication

For Expressives: Demonstrate high energy when working with this co-worker
–Pick up the pace
–Focus on the big picture
–Say what you feel, be candid and direct
–Facilitate this person's self-determination
–Provide some discipline around use of time

For Analyticals: Be task-oriented when working with this co-worker
–De-emphasize feelings
–Emphasize facts and details
–Be systematic
–Be well-organized
–Use less small talk
–Follow through on your commitments

Analyticals

For fellow Analyticals: Like you, this co-worker has the need to be accurate
–Do not get bogged down in detail
–Help this person reach decisions
–Encourage big-picture thinking
–Encourage risk-taking

For Drivers: Focus on needed conclusions and outcomes
–Pick up the pace
–Demonstrate sufficient energy
–Provide clear options
–Don't get bogged down in details or theory

For Expressives: Demonstrate high energy with this co-worker
–Make personal contact
–Pick up the pace
–Allow feelings and opinions to be expressed
–Allow for some fun and spontaneity
–Recognize this person's contributions

For Amiables: Make genuine personal contact with this co-worker
–Focus more on feelings
–Offer assistance regarding work to be done
–Provide a structure with an emphasis on people
–Don't overdo facts and logic
–Pay attention to relationships

Table 8.6.
Board Team Phases and Roles and Chairperson/Leader Behavior and Style

Phases of Teamwork	Team Roles	Behavior	Style
Forming	Conductor, Consensus Builder, Resource Seeker	Directing	Driver
Storming	Idea Generator, Checker	Coaching	Expressive
Norming	Implementer	Supporting	Amiable
Performing	Change Advocate, Arbiter	Delegating	Analytical

- *Supporting:* The chairperson allows members to make decisions about task allocation and processes. The board members all have control, but the chairperson acts as a facilitator.
- *Delegating:* The chairperson is still involved in making decisions, but control is with the board team as a whole. The team decides when and how the chairperson will be involved, and the chairperson merely monitors performance and progress.

In their latest publication, Hersey, Blanchard, and Johnson reference the linkage with these other models.[5] As you can see in table 8.6, the leadership of the board and the leadership of the business bring the same behaviors into play. For example, when a board or business team is being formed, a conductor needs to come forward and direct the actions of others—a driving leadership style. Once the board gets through its orientation stage or the business through its start-up phase, the leader needs to be open to the ideas of others while still acting as a "reality check." The leader also needs to act as a coach that energizes rather than demotivates others. This is an expressive leadership style in action. As the success of the board and business grows, the leader should support and empower others through an amiable leadership style that values relationships. Finally, when the board and business reach maturity, the analytical leader can delegate authority to others but still remain as a power that can arbitrate and influence change.

The Lead Independent Director

There is an ongoing debate in the United States about who should be the chairman of the board. At this writing, 54% of the chairmanships of U.S. firms was held by the CEO. Andrew Kakabadse and Nada Kakabadse offer a harsh assessment of the U.S. chairmen: "On the one hand, the best American companies have world-class chairmen. Yet, on the other, in the vast majority of U.S. firms, the quality of the chairmen is mediocre at best."[6] They offer a board performance assessment and a more extensive Chairman Audit checklist as a basis for their conclusion.

To their point, the chairman/CEO combination has such a heavy load of responsibilities that it is difficult to imagine one person having the time or inclination to consider and manage the behavioral dynamics of the board team. The *Agenda's* 2009 Board Leadership Guide reports that since 2004, the number of boards with lead directors has increased by 64%. At this writing, there is greater pressure from stakeholders (including congressional leaders), to separate the chairmanship from the CEO. A Lead Independent Director (LID) as chair of the board is a viable alternative.

If a board is not going to split the roles of chairman and CEO, the Lead Independent Director (LID) is still the best candidate to lead the board in its processes. The partnership of Jack Krol, LID, and Ed Breen, CEO, at Tyco International is an example of how productive separating the roles can be. Teamwork was something they approached deliberately and thoughtfully, as can be read in Tyco's "How we conduct ourselves" document: "We foster an environment that encourages innovation, creativity and results through teamwork and mutual respect. We practice leadership that teaches, inspires and promotes full participation and career development. We encourage open and effective communication and interaction."[7] This statement guided the dynamics both in the boardroom and in the business.

The Council of Institutional Investors clearly delineates what the duties of a LID include:

- Presiding at all meetings of the board at which the chairman is not present, including executive sessions of the independent directors.
- Serving as liaison between the chairman and the independent directors.
- Approving information sent to the board.
- Approving meeting agendas for the board.

- Approving meeting schedules to assure that there is sufficient time for discussion of all agenda items.
- Having the authority to call meetings of the independent directors.
- Being available for consultation and direct communication, if requested by major shareholders.[8]

As I see this momentum grow for a greater leadership role for the LID, I am recommending the addition of another duty to improve the board's effectiveness:

- Serving as the process leader for the board.

The Chief Process Leader

Although the duties of the LID may seem daunting at first, what I've offered in this chapter can help a newly appointed LID manage and strengthen the board's dynamics.

- **Know Yourself:** Assess your board's Stage of Development (Forming, Storming, Norming, Performing), and you and your fellow board members' primary, secondary, and least preferred team roles.
- **Control Yourself:** Know your limitations and call on the strengths of other members to advance the board team's development.
- **Know Others:** Assess the Social Styles of each member of the board, both its external and internal directors.
- **Do Something for Others:** Be responsive to each member's need and orientation in the boardroom.
- **Be the Chief Process Leader (CPL):** Employ the behavior (Directing, Coaching, Supporting, Delegating) needed by the board to increase its effectiveness.

Effective board dynamics do not occur by chance. Team success requires an effective process leader just as much as business success requires an effective CEO. If boards are to going to face up to the challenges of being the CEO's boss, a process leader is necessary to help facilitate an effective partnership between the board and its CEO. The LID as the CPL will not only strengthen the board's teamwork, but become the trusted partner of fellow directors and the CEO.

Outstanding Directors

This book addresses the need to form a powerful partnership between directors and their CEO's. Outstanding Directors Exchange (ODX) recognizes directors each year who have exerted their leadership in the boardroom and achieved a productive partnership with their CEO's.

The ODX Outstanding Directors Program honors independent directors of public companies who have been recognized by their peers for making a courageous or valuable contribution to the companies on whose boards they serve. Since its inception in 1998 the program has honored more than 80 corporate directors of American public companies. The Criteria for Outstanding Directors are

- Has consistently made strong contributions to corporate boards.
- Has been a key player during important periods in a company's growth or transition.
- Has a deep interest in the company's business.
- Demonstrates business savvy.
- Devotes time to the job, both inside and outside the boardroom.
- Is compatible but forthright; speaks up to challenge management's assumptions.
- Demonstrates judgment and discretion that the CEO trusts and respects.
- Is admired by fellow directors for courage, integrity, and consensus-building skills.
- Is clearly aligned with interest of shareholders.[9]

Many of these criteria touch on the partnership and leadership strategies I've discussed throughout this book. Attention to growth and transitions entails an awareness of the business cycle and how to adapt to it; interest in the company's business requires an understanding of the company's strategic context and intent; and compatibility and forthrightness indicate a concern with appropriate leadership styles and an ability to express tough love.

I attended the dinners where these 2008 directors were honored for their contribution, and I listened attentively for those leadership qualities that affirm my model and methods of tough love in the boardroom.

• **Steven F. Goldstone**, retired chairman/CEO, RJR Nabisco. Public directorships: American Standard, ConAgra Foods, Greenhill & Co., Merck (effective April 2008). Goldstone was an OD honoree for successfully guiding ConAgra and American Standard (now Trane) through major business restructurings. Goldstone set a new agenda for growth and facilitated a successful search for a new CEO. At the ceremony, retired KPMG chairman and CEO Steve Butler said of Goldstone, "Steve has been instrumental in working with management to map ConAgra's current course. The board decided to split the chairman and CEO roles and it is easy to see why Steve is chairman." Goldstone's success is evidence of the power of an LID assuming a greater leadership role on the board. Working in partnership with the new CEO to set an agenda for change and growth reinforces the first step in achieving CEO alignment: Understand and affirm the Strategic Context and Intent. (See chapter 6.)

• **Harvey Golub,** retired chairman/CEO, American Express. Public directorships: Campbell Soup, Dow Jones (1997–2007). Golub was honored for leadership that resulted in a major business turnaround at Campbell Soup. In 2000, shareholders were questioning the company's ability to stay independent. Under Golub's chairmanship, a successful CEO change followed by intense product innovation and marketing investment reinvigorated the company and the share price. Another LID, Golub took steps in exerting tough love in the boardroom by making an obvious attempt to "match the organization's need with the leadership that is required." (See chapter 2.)

• **Judith R. Haberkorn,** retired president, Consumer Sales, Verizon Communications. Public directorships: Armstrong World Industries, Computer Sciences Corporation, ExpressJet Holdings. Haberkorn was honored for her role in helping postbankruptcy MCI regain viability and respectability. She joined the board in 2004 when WorldCom—by then a synonym for bad governance—emerged from bankruptcy. A veteran of bankruptcy workouts, reorganizations, and leadership development, Haberkorn helped CEO Michael Cappellas and the board to get back on track by installing new management, restoring stability, and promoting a sorely needed culture of ethics and honesty from the top down. In doing so, she brought to the forefront the first standard of a Social Contract for the company: commitment to values. (See chapter 1.) Rebranded as MCI, the company was sold to Verizon in 2006 for $8.5 billion after a highly publicized bidding war with Qwest Communications.

- **William R. Holland,** retired chairman/CEO, United Dominion Industries. Public directorships: Enpro Industries, Goodrich, Lanc. Holland was an OD honoree for building success into Goodrich's spin-off of Enpro Industries. He successfully mentored a first-time CEO, put together a strong board, and helped turn a $5 stock into a $40 one, creating tremendous value for shareholders. In mentoring his CEO, Holland became a trusted advisor and adhered to the fifth standard of the Social Contract: commitment to coaching for their continuous improvement. (See chapter 1.) Given the company's success, I suspect that Holland gave his CEO feedback on his leadership and made sure that he understood the state of the business at all times. In this case, the soft metrics of this partnership were linked to success in the hard metrics of the business. (See chapter 4.)

- **Elizabeth Kennan**, president emeritus, Mount Holyoke College. Public directorship: Northeast Utilities. Kennan was recognized for being a model lead director during troubled times at Northeast Utilities. A 28-year veteran of the Northeast board, Liz was a lead director before the phrase was even coined. In the 1990s, amidst public outcry about alleged cozy relationships with regulators and an anti-whistle-blowing culture, Kennan took a head-on approach to the issues of nuclear power plant safety. Under her leadership, the board embraced the need for greater vigilance, eventually pleading guilty to numerous violations, paying a hefty fine, and enduring three years of probation. Today Northeast Utilities is a robust, fully regulated utility that is well positioned to capture the burgeoning electricity market from New York to Boston. Liz Kennan's leadership behavior models the second standard of the Social Contract, a "Commitment to the Stakeholders: Customers, Employees, Shareholders, and Community" not just in word, but in deed. (See chapter 1.) This commitment was recognized by the *New York Times*'s Gretchen Morgenson, who opened her column in August of 2006 with, "Let us now praise a mutual fund company that actually voted in its customers' interests when casting annual proxy votes this spring."

- **Bernard G. Rethore**, chairman emeritus and retired CEO of Flowserve. Independent director: Belden, Dover, Mueller Water Products, and Walter Industries. Rethore was recognized for ensuring that the sale of Maytag earned the highest possible return for shareholders. He was a director at Maytag from 1994 until the company's sale to Whirlpool in 2006. Former Maytag chairman and CEO Ralph Hake said of Rethore, "Bernie was a superb director who kept shareholder value at the top of his list. In rough numbers, the final price tag was $270 million higher than the initial bid. An outstanding premium, indeed." Like Kennan, Rethore displayed an adherence to the second standard of the Social Contract: Commitment to the stakeholders. (See chapter 1.)

• **Charles R. Lee,** retired chairman/CEO, Verizon Public directorships: DIRECTV, Marathon Oil, Proctor & Gamble, United Technologies, US Steel. Lee was an OD honoree for the motivating and transparent CEO compensation plan he championed at DIRECTV. Lee helped developed this package for a high-performing CEO in a very competitive marketplace, all the while dealing with a complex ownership structure that included keeping Rupert Murdoch and Sumner Redstone in the loop. Former CBS CEO Peter Lund applauded Lee at the ceremony, saying, "Chuck drove a very transparent, inclusive, shareholder-friendly process that created a compensation scheme that will stand up to anyone's scrutiny. He is as good a director as I've ever seen." In doing so, Lee models the fourth standard of the Social Contract: a commitment to transparency through complete honesty in financial and nonfinancial matters. (See chapter 1.) With the recent uproar concerning executive compensation, his leadership practice is more relevant today than ever before for Board Compensation Committee members.

I will continue to study what makes individuals like these outstanding and, in so doing, try to confirm and revise my understanding of the role of the Social Contract, tough love, and my ILM. It is my belief that boards must take these ideas into account in order to successfully fulfill their role as their CEO's boss.

Conclusion

This book is intended to help boards operate more effectively as the boss of the CEO—from selecting the right CEO, to establishing a working relationship and giving effective feedback. The core argument is that the CEO's style needs to be matched to the business at each point in its cycle and that the board needs to intervene actively to help the CEO close any gaps between their capabilities/style and the requirement of the company.

Although attention to leadership styles and a commitment to tough love all make sense on paper, implementing these strategies in the midst of the business cycle is sometimes difficult. During a downturn, attention is often on immediate solutions rather than on overall strategies, and during an upturn it can feel irrelevant to examine a system or partnership that seems to be working. However, because of the changing nature of the business cycle, it is imperative that boards constantly evaluate their leadership and their strategy. The method I've presented can help boards and businesses at every stage of the business cycle and can help regulate one of the most important relationships in the company: the relationship between the board and its CEO. Although the theories behind my method are important, they come with concrete practices that any board can and should implement:

- **Develop your Social Contract.** A board/CEO partnership cannot be sustained by good intentions alone; it must be defined by an explicit statement of the beliefs and behaviors that are essential for the general will of the organization. Boards should share a set of common commitments with their CEO:

  - Commitment to values: a leadership credo that answers the question, "What do we stand for as an organization?"
  - Commitment to the stakeholders—customers, employees, shareholders, and community.
  - Commitment to risk assessment—a willingness to manage the company's risk profile.
  - Commitment to transparency—complete honesty in financial and nonfinancial matters.
  - Commitment to coaching for their continuous improvement.

- **Practice tough love.** Intentionally address the realities of your CEO's tenure with the appropriate amount of tough love before your company and CEO become dysfunctional. Boards can learn from those who study CEO tenure, company performance, and successful leadership behaviors. Taking this research into account can help the company thrive at every stage in the life cycle of the business.
- **Constantly assess your CEO's leadership agenda, practices, and style.** Business cycles are unavoidable and uncertain, and the board needs to face this reality and be prepared to change its leadership if the CEO cannot adjust to the changing conditions.
- **Develop the hard and soft metrics that link your CEO's leadership practices to the organization's needs.** The board needs to repeatedly measure what it wants done and reward what it wants its CEO to get done.
- **Investigate the behavior of your prospective CEO during both good and bad times, and always be aware of the biases that can cloud your judgment.** There is no short-cut to making an informed choice about a new CEO.

- Assume that your team dynamics will be influenced by the stage of the board's development, the mix of its member's styles, and the leadership behavior your directors will employ. In addition, accept that your credibility with your shareholders will be based on their perception of the independence of your external directors from the CEO and the internal directors on your board.

By employing these models and methods, the board and the CEO can work together productively and efficiently to keep the company on track.

My Continuing Commitment

My work as Columbia's faculty director of ODX provided me with the face validity for this model and method for helping boards operate more effectively in their role as boss of the CEO. I intend to continue to examine the leadership practices of the Outstanding Directors of ODX and to test the book's content further in one of a series of corporate governance programs that are being designed for board directors to be offered by Columbia Executive Education in conjunction with ODX. Our intent is to continue to bring theory to practice and to help boards, CEO's, and businesses succeed.

Epilogue

2020 Foresight

Zeitgeist: the ideas prevalent in a period and place

If business marketing à la "Mad Men" was king in the 1950s and 1960s, and finance ruled the second half of the century, then the failures of Enron, WorldCom, Global Crossing, Tyco, Adelphia, and Rite Aid have made corporate governance the major concern of the new millennium. With the current economic crisis has come a crisis of confidence in corporate governance, which is facing scrutiny and, as a consequence, inevitable change. As we reach the end of a tumultuous decade, a natural question is, "What will the next decade bring?"

In 2002, the NYSE and NASDAQ Corporate Accountability and Listing Standards Committees published a list of recommendations for changes in the exchange's listing requirements to enhance corporate governance in the aftermath of the "meltdown" of companies caused by failures of diligence, ethics, and controls.[1] The recommendations, listed in table Epi.1, attempted to enhance the independence of independent directors and as a consequence emphasize their role as the "CEO's boss."

Corporate governance faces more government intervention now than ever—from President Obama's administration, the U.S. Congress, and the SEC. Whereas Sarbanes-Oxley was established to ensure financial accuracy in what was being reported, these actions portend even more systemic and comprehensive changes in the practice of corporate governance.

Table Epi.1.
NYSE and NASDAQ Recommendations

Selected Final Recommendations of NYSE Corporate Accountability and Listing Standards Committee	Selected Final Recommendations of NASDAQ Corporate Accountability and Listing Standards Committee
Independent directors must comprise a majority of a board.	Majority of board members will be independent.
All currently listed companies will be required to achieve majority-independence within 24 months of this rule's enactment. Companies newly listed must comply within 24 months.	NASDAQ will require a company to modify the composition of its board of directors immediately following its first annual meeting that is at least 120 days after SEC approval of the changes.
Companies must have a nominating committee, compensation committee (or committees of the company's own denomination with the same responsibilities) and an audit committee, each comprised solely of independent directors.	All director nominations must be approved by an independent nominations committee or by a majority of the independent directors.
	Executive officer compensation must be approved by an independent compensation committee or by a majority of the independent directors.
	One nonindependent director may be allowed to serve on compensation or nomination committees under certain disclosed circumstances.
***	***
For a director to be deemed "independent," the board must affirmatively determine that he or she has no material relationship with the listed company.	Further tightening of the definition of *independence*, which excludes large shareholders, relatives of executives, and employees of the outside auditor.
***	***
Independence also requires a 5-year "cooling-off" period for former employees of the listed company or of its independent auditor; for former employees of any company whose compensation committee includes an officer of the listed company; and for immediate family members of the above.	Establish a 3-year cooling-off period for all nonindependent directors before they can be considered independent.
***	***
Shareholders must be given the opportunity to vote on all stock option plans, except employment-inducement options, option plans acquired through mergers and tax-qualified plans such as ESOPs and 401(k)s.	Consistent with the recommendations of the president, NASDAQ will require shareholder approval for all stock option plans.
	Existing exemptions for ESOP and inducement options will be retained.
***	***

Listed companies must publish codes of business conduct and ethics, and key committee charters. Waivers for directors or executive officers must be promptly disclosed.

Each listed company's CEO must certify annually that he or she is not aware of any violation by the company of NYSE corporate-governance standards.

All companies must have codes of conduct that

☐ Address conflicts of interest and compliance with applicable laws;

☐ Employ enforcement mechanisms;

☐ Disclose waivers to officers/directors;

☐ Are publicly available

***

***

The NYSE urges every listed company to establish an orientation program for new board members.

The board indicated the desire for companies to require continuing education for all directors.

The *Agenda* newsletter reported on the pending initiatives listed in table Epi.2 just six months into the legislative term.[2]

The CEO and the Board

An effective partnership between the board and its CEO is the first step on the path to good corporate governance in the next decade. To achieve their shared goals, external directors will need to assert their fiduciary role and CEO's will need to practice executive leadership. It will take more time to forge a partnership and more time to maintain an alliance than in the past. Shareholder activism will continue to increase in direct proportion to the performance of the enterprise.

One of the most productive board/CEO partnerships I experienced in my four decades in higher education was at the College of New Jersey, where I served as the chief student affairs officer. Erna Hoover was chairperson of the board of trustees when it appointed Harold Eickhoff as the new president in 1980. Eickhoff and the board forged a partnership to transform the college from a "competitive" state college to one of the nation's "best buys" and "most selective" comprehensive colleges. In a recent interview, I asked Dr. Eickhoff what made this partnership work. His statement was, "Noses in, hands off."

Table Epi.2.
Governance Reform

		House	Senate	
What the major players in changing corporate governance are pushing for				
	Obama	(Peter's bill)	(Schumer's bill)	SEC
Annual Elections			X	
Majority Voting		X	X	
Proxy Access		X	X	X
Broker-Vote Ban		X		X
Independent Chairs		X	X	
Shareholders' Say on Pay	X	X	X	
Shareholders' Say on Golden Parachutes			X	
Comp Consulate Independence	X	X		X
Clawbacks		X		
No Severance for Poor Performance*		X		
Improved Disclosure of Performance Goals	X	X		

Reprinted with permission from Marc Hogan's "In a Tale of Three Proposals, House Bill Goes Furthest," *Agenda*, June 22, 2009. All Rights Reserved.
*The Obama administration's principles on executive compensation state that golden parachutes should be examined to ensure they align with shareholder interests.

During an ODX session in 2009 entitled "The CEO and the Board: Forging an Effective Partnership," I heard this same bromide spoken more than once. Eric Wiserman, chairman and CEO of VF; Tim Eller, chairman and CEO of Centex; and Andrea Jung, chairman and CEO of Avon, were on the panel. They cautioned that effective partnerships don't occur by chance, but take concentrated time and effort. They stressed that the board/CEO relationship needs to be an ongoing agenda item addressed through open and honest communication, transparency, and the building of trust. Ursie Fairbairn, 2009 Outstanding Director, facilitated the panel discussion, and, as a director at Centrix and VF, she could speak firsthand to the wisdom of this partnership principle. In short, directors assert their fiduciary role and CEO's their executive leadership.

CORPORATE GOVERNANCE PREDICTIONS
FOR THE NEXT DECADE (2010–2020)

1. *Boards will become more egalitarian, participatory, and regulated.* Shareholder activism will continue to expand the slate of director nominees. As a result, board membership will be open to more individuals than in the past. These newly constituted boards will be known for the full participation of all its members—no "free riders." However, the activities of the board will be more regulated by the governance reform measures.

2. *Directors will "run" for a seat on the board, not dissimilar to a political election.* The aspiring directors will need to go beyond being vetted by the governance committee and accepting their nomination to the board. Directors will need to campaign, as any candidate would for public office. The CEO's will no longer be able to "anoint" without election or discussion—the days of the corporate "party boss" are over.

3. *Shareholders will have input in deciding the best board chairperson.* Shareholders will want a say on who should chair their board of directors. Savvy CEO's will openly solicit the feelings of the company's significant shareholders, as well as the independent directors, before assuming that they should be the one to fill that seat at the table. As a result, the number of nonexecutive chairpersons will increase in the coming decade.

4. *Lead independent directors will become the chief process leaders of their boards.* For boards to be highly functioning teams, process leaders need to attend to the group's dynamics. The tasks of the board will be managed by the chairperson, but the relationship will be managed by the lead independent director. CEO's will rely on this chief process leader to help them forge an effective partnership.

5. *The strategic risk profile will be a recurring item on the board's regular agenda.* The risk profile of the company will be the work of a committee-of-the-whole of the board. Strategic risk will be a standing agenda for its regular meetings. Shareholders will demand that

their treasure is being wisely invested in the business and not at risk
due to inadequate oversight.

Concluding Thought

When CEO's derail, the whole company feels the crash. By stepping up to
the role of the CEO's boss, the board can help the CEO make the right decisions for the business and can show "tough love" when it's time to align
the leadership agenda, practices, and style with the current cycle of the
business. By heeding these predictions and the strategies delineated in this
book for strengthening the relationship between the board and the CEO,
companies have a chance of making the next decade more successful than
the last.

NOTES

1. The Social Contract

1. D. K. Berman, "Where Was Lehman's Board?" *The Wall Street Journal*, September 15, 2008.

2. Tyco International, "Our History." http://www.tyco-emp.com/OurHistory_6462.aspx (accessed August 23, 2009).

3. Tyco International Ltd., "Press Release: Tyco Announces Intent to Separate into Three Publicly Traded Companies," January 13, 2006. http://tyco.mediaroom.com/index.php?year=2006&s=43 (accessed August 23, 2009).

4. Tyco International Ltd., "Board Governance Principles: Amended December 6, 2007." http://www.tyco.com/wps/wcm/connect/7ec1ae004d67be70bdc3ff790dc56802/Board+Governance+Principles.pdf?MOD=AJPERES (accessed September 8, 2009).

5. ODX. "Outstanding Directors: Jack Krol." http://www.theodx.com/outstandingdirectors/061107_Od_Profile_Krol_Email.pdf (accessed September 18, 2009).

6. Lawrence Kohlberg, *Essays on Moral Development*, vol. I (San Francisco: Harper & Row, 1981), 409–12.

7. G. A. Miller, "The Magical Number Seven, Plus or Minus Two: Some Limits on Our Capacity for Processing Information," *Psychological Review* 63 (1956): 81–97.

8. Johnson & Johnson, "Our Credo Values." http://www.jnj.com/connect/about-jnj/jnj-credo(accessed September 10, 2009).

9. Johnson & Johnson, "Our Credo." http://www.jnj.com/wps/wcm/connect/30e290804ae70eb4bc4afc0f0a50cff8/our-credo.pdf?MOD=AJPERES (accessed September 10, 2009).

10. M&T Bank, "Vision Statement." https://www.mtb.com/ABOUTUS/Pages/VisionStatement.aspx (accessed September 8, 2009).

11. M&T Bank. "In the Community." https://www.mtb.com/aboutus/community/Pages/Index.aspx (accessed September 8, 2009).

12. Jennifer Reingold, "Banking the Buffalo Way," *Fortune*, April 17, 2009.

13. Berman, "Where Was Lehman's Board?"

14. Michael E. Raynor, *The Strategy Paradox: Why Committing to Success Leads Companies to Failure, and What to Do About It* (New York: Doubleday, 2007).

2. Tough Love in the Boardroom

1. Lehman Brothers, "Mission Statement," http://www.lehman.com/who/mission (accessed January 10, 2008).

2. Lehman Brothers, "Sustainability Principles," http://www.lehman.com/who/sustainability (accessed January 10, 2008).

3. Carl Icahn, "The Icahn Report." http://www.icahnreport.com (accessed October 13, 2008).

4. Charles Beach and Nell Minow. "Risk Management: An Oversight Oversight," March 1, 2009. http://www.risk.net/public/showPage.html?page=printer_friendly_risknet&print=843572 (accessed September 11, 2009).

5. Yalman Onoran and John Helyar, "Fuld Sought Buffett Offer He Refused as Lehman Sank." November 10, 2008. http://www.bloomberg.com/apps/news?pid=20601109&refer=home&sid=aMQJV3iJ5M8c (accessed September 11, 2009).

6. Ibid.

7. David W. Merrill and Roger H. Reid, *Personal Styles and Effective Performance* (Boca Raton: CRC, 1981).

8. CNN Online. "CEO Roberto C. Goizueta Dies at 65." October 18, 1997. http://www.cnn.com/US/9710/18/goizueta.obit (accessed September 11, 2009).

9. Natasha Tarpley, "What Really Happened at Coke?" *Fortune*, January 10, 2000. http://money.cnn.com/magazines/fortune/fortune_archive/2000/01/10/271736/index.htm (accessed September 11, 2009).

10. Betsy McKay et al., "Tone Deaf: Ivester Had All Skills of a CEO but One: Ear for Political Nuance—Clumsy Handling of One Flap After Another Cost Him Coke Board's Confidence—How to Irritate the Europeans," *The Wall Street Journal*, December 17, 1999.

11. Tyco International Ltd., "Board Governance Principles: Amended December 6, 2007." http://www.tyco.com/wps/wcm/connect/7ec1ae004d67be70bdc3ff790dc56802/Board+Governance+Principles.pdf?MOD=AJPERES.

12. James M. Kouzes and Barry Z. Posner, *The Leadership Challenge: How to Get Extraordinary Things Done in Organizations* (San Francisco: Jossey-Bass, 1987).

13. Onoran and Helyar, "Fuld Sought Buffett. . . ."

14. Donald C. Hambrick and Gregory D. S. Fukutomi, "The Seasons of a CEO's Tenure," *The Academy of Management Review,* Vol. 16, No. 4 (Oct, 1991), pp. 719–742.

15. James C. Collins, *How the Mighty Fall: And Why Some Companies Never Give In* (New York: HarperCollins, 2009).

16. Onoran and Helyar, "Fuld Sought Buffett. . . ."

17. D. K. Berman, "Where Was Lehman's Board?" *The Wall Street Journal,* September 15, 2008.

18. JetBlue. "Overview," 2002 Annual Report. http://www.jetblue.com/about/ourcompany/annualreport/2002/about-main.html (accessed September 11, 2009).

19. Ibid.

20. Nancy Brown Johnson, "Low-Cost Competition in the United States." Labor and Employment Relations Association Series, Proceedings of the 58th Annual Meeting. 2006. http://www.lera.uiuc.edu/pubs/proceedings/index.html (accessed September 11, 2009).

21. George Will, "An Airline that Isn't Bankrupt." *The Washington Post,* January 25, 2007.

22. Neeleman, February 2006, jetblue.com.

23. Press release, February 14, 2007, jetblue.com.

24. Allan Sloan, "From One Case Study to Another," *The Washington Post,* February 27, 2007.

25. Press release, May 10, 2007, jetblue.com.

26. JetBlue. Annual Report 2007. http://library.corporate-ir.net/library/13/131/131045/items/290628/JBLU_2007annualreport.pdf (September 11, 2009).

27. Ibid.

3. Why the Right Partnership Matters

1. Noel Capon, *Key Account Management and Planning: The Comprehensive Handbook for Managing Your Company's Most Important Strategic Asset* (New York: Free Press, 2001).

2. Capon, *Key Account Management and Planning,* p. 111.

3. Jack Welch and Suzy Welch, *Winning* (New York: HarperCollins, 2005).

4. Jacqueline Durett, "GE Hones Its Leaders at Crotonville," *Monday,* May 1, 2006. Training.

5. Larry Bossidy and Ram Charan, *Execution: The Discipline of Getting Things Done* (New York: Crown Business, 2002).

6. T. Chapelle, "Directors in Dark Have Themselves to Blame," *Agenda* 27 (May 2008).

7. M. Beer and N. Nohria, eds., *Breaking the Code of Change* (Cambridge: Harvard Business School Press, 2000).

8. W. Warner Burke, *Organization Change: Theory and Practice* (Thousand Oaks, CA: Sage, 2002).

4. Leadership Metrics

1. R. Charan, *Boards That Deliver* (Hoboken, NJ: John Wiley & Sons, 2005).

2. M. Fenlon, *The Leadership Compass* (Vector Data Systems, 2001).

3. Ibid.

4. W. Klepper, "What Effective CEOs Have Yet to Learn," *Effective Executive*. January 2009, ICFAI.

5. P. Drucker, "What Makes an Effective Executive?" *Harvard Business Review*, June 2004.

6. P. Honey and A. Mumford, *The Learning Styles Helper's Guide* (Berkshire, UK: Peter Honey Publications, 2000).

7. Ibid.

8. Edward E. Lawler III, *Talent: Making People Your Competitive Advantage* (Hoboken, NJ: Jossey-Bass, 2008).

9. E. E. Lawler, "Good Riddance to the Imperial CEO," *Business Week*, October 24, 2008.

10. M. Hogan, "Where Did Lehman's Board Go Wrong?" *Agenda*, September 22, 2008.

11. Y. Onaran and J. Helyar, *Fuld Sought Buffett Offer He Refused as Lehman Sank*. November 10, 2008, Bloomberg.

12. S. Kirchgaessner and G. Farrell, "Fuld Breaks Silence on Lehman Collapse," *Financial Times*. October 7, 2008.

13. Hogan, "Where Did Lehman's Board Go Wrong?"

5. How the Partnership Can Go Wrong: TTWO

1. S. Siverthorne, "Managing the Gamer Generation," in *Working Knowledge for Business Leaders*. 10/18/2004, Harvard Business School. http://hbswk.hbs.edu/archive/4429.html

2. Take-Two Interactive Software, I., *10 KSB Annual Report*, February 6, 1998. http://www.secinfo.com/dr6wd.73k.htm

3. G. Marcial, "Take-Two Gets a Second Chance," *BusinessWeek Online*, December 19, 2001.

4. M. Richtel, "Thicket of Ties in Management at Game Maker Raises Doubts," *The New York Times*, May 12, 2003.

5. Take-Two Interactive Software, I, *Annual Report*, 2003.

6. Take-Two Interactive Software, I, "Take-Two Interactive Software, Inc. Reports Fourth Quarter and Fiscal 2007 Financial Results; Fourth Quarter Bottom Line Exceeds Guidance; Net Loss Declines on Revenue Growth and Reduced Expenses; Company Reiterates Fiscal Year 2008 Guidance and Provides First Quarter Guidance" December 18, 2007, business wire.

7. "Take-Two Coup a Governance Win," *Associated Press Digital*, March 31, 2007.

8. D. Beim, Fraud, Backdating, Activist Coup! Take Two Interactive: A Case Study. Unpublished work: presented at ODX as a case study in New York City in 2007.

6. What Directors Need to Know Before Committing to a CEO

1. D. C. Hambrick and J. W. Fredrickson, "Are You Sure You Have a Strategy?" *Academy of Management Executive*, 15, no. 4 (2001).

2. M. Tushman and C. O'Reilly, *Managerial Problem Solving: A Congruence Approach* (Cambridge: Harvard Business Publishing, 2007).

3. R. G. McGrath and I. C. MacMillan, *MarketBusters: 40 Strategic Moves That Drive Exceptional Business Growth* (Cambridge: Harvard Business School Press, 2005).

4. W. Pietersen, *Reinventing Strategy: Using Strategic Learning to Create and Sustain Breakthrough Performance* (Hoboken, NJ: John Wiley & Sons, 2002).

5. W. Pietersen, "Strategic Learning." http://williepietersen.com/learning/learning.asp# (accesed September 14, 2009).

6. Pietersen, *Reinventing Strategy*.

7. IKEA. "The Ikea Way." http://www.ikea.com/ms/en_US/about_ikea/the_ikea_way/index.htm (accesed September 14, 2009).

8. Tushman and O'Reilly, *Managerial Problem Solving*.

9. W. G. Bowen, *The Board Book: An Insider's Guide for Directors and Trustees* (New York: Norton, 2008).

10. Ewing Township New Jersey, *About Ewing*. 2008. http://ewingnj.org/

11. Jersey, State of New, *New Jersey Core Curriculum Content Standards*, Department of Education, State of New Jersey, May 1996.

12. Schools, T.E.P., *Philosophy and Belief Statements*, November 11, 2002, The Ewing Public Schools, Ewing, NJ.

13. N. L. Arnez, "The Impact of Black Women in Education: An Historical Overview of Selected Black Female Superintendents of Public School Systems," *The Journal of Negro Education* (Summer 1982): 309–17

14. R. B. Cialdini, "Harnessing the Science of Persuasion," *Harvard Business Review* (October 2001).

7. The Board's Commitment to the CEO

1. Ram Charan, *Boards That Deliver: Advancing Corporate Governance from Compliance to Competitive Advantage* (San Francisco: Jossey-Bass, 2005), 88–90.

2. Richard M. Steinberg and Catherine L. Bromilow, *Corporate Governance—What Works Best* (Altamonte, FL: Institute of Internal Auditors Research Foundation, 2000).

8. Effective Board Dynamics

1. Bruce Tuckman, "Developmental Sequence in Small Groups," *Psychological Bulletin* 63 (1965): 384–99.

2. Pablo Cardona and Helen Wilkinson, "Team Work," IESE Business School, University of Navarra, Occasional Paper no. 07/10-E (December 2006).

3. R. Meredeith Belbin, *Management Teams: Why They Succeed or Fail* (London: Heinemann, 1981).

4. Daniel Goleman, *Social Intelligence: The New Science of Social Relationships* (New York: Bantam Books, 2006). Also by Goleman: *Emotional Intelligence: Why It Can Matter More Than IQ* (New York: Bantam, 1996).

5. Paul Hersey, Kenneth H. Blanchard, Dewey E. Johnson, *Management of Organizational Behavior,* 9th ed. (Upper Saddle River, NJ: Prentice Hall, 2008).

6. Andrew Kakabadse and Nada Kakabadse, *Learning the Board: The Six Principles of World Class Chairmen* (New York: Palgrave Macmillan, 2008).

7. Tyco International, "Our Vision and Values." http://www.tyco.com/wps/wcm/connect/7ec1ae004d67be70bdc3ff790dc56802/Board+Governance+Principles.pdf ?MOD=AJPERES (accessed September 17, 2009).

8. Correspondence between Thomas P. Lemke and Ann Yerger. http://www.cii .org/UserFiles/file/resource%20center/majority%20votes/mv%202007%20PDFs/Legg %20Mason.PDF (accessed September 17, 2009).

9. ODX. "Outstanding Directors: Selection Process." http://www.theodx.com/ outstandingdirectors/odprocess.php (accessed September 18, 2009).

Epilogue

1. NYSE. New York Stock Exchange Corporate Accountability and Listing Standards Committee. June 6, 2002. http://www.iasplus.com/resource/nysegovf.pdf. September 18, 2009.

2. Marc Hogan, In Tale of Three Proposals, House Bill Goes Furthest. *Agenda,* June 22, 2009.

INDEX

needs, organizational, 18–20
Neeleman, David, 25–28, 39, 43
norming, 103, 114
NYSE (New York Stock Exchange), 123–25

Obama, Barack, 123
ODX (Outstanding Directors Exchange), 2–3, 4, 11, 53–54, 117
Open Skies, 25
O'Reilly, C., 77

Palmer, Doug, 81
partnership, board/CEO, 30–44, 58–68; effective, 1–3, 5–6, 7, 125, 126; failures in, 10, 16, 58, 64–65, 67; and feedback, 5–7, 89, 90, 92–94; and leadership, 1, 11, 59–65; and metrics, 89–90, 100; and Social Contract, 5–7, 9–10, 94, 121
Pastino, Albert, 63
people, 77, 78, 80, 82
performance, 45, 79
performing, 103, 114
persuasion, 85–87
Pettit, Christopher, 20
pharmaceutical industry, 7–8
Pietersen, Willie, 71
Posner, Barry Z., 19, 31
problem solving, 69–70
processes, 77, 80; for alignment, 70–71; of Social Contract, 11–13
Ptak, Thomas, 60, 61

Ras, Barbara A., 60, 61
Raynor, Michael, 9
reciprocity, 85, 111
Redstone, Sumner, 120
Reed, Roger, 17, 31, 106, 107, 110, 111
Reinventing Strategy: Using Strategic Learning to Create and Sustain Breakthrough Performance (Pietersen), 71
resource seeker, 104, 114
responsibility, 3–4, 6, 7, 12, 47
responsiveness, 31–32

Rethore, Bernard G., 119
return on assets (ROA), 45
return on equity (ROE), 45
return on investment (ROI), 45
revenue per available seat mile (RASM), 26
rewards, 56, 60, 98, 100
risk assessment, 5, 12; commitment to, 9, 60, 88, 121
risk management, 9, 12, 15–16, 98, 100
risk/reward ratios, 24
Roedel, Richard, 65
root-cause analysis, 94–96, 98
Rousseau, Jean-Jacques, 1

S curves, 22–24, 42, 44
Sarbanes-Oxley Act, 123
SEC (Securities and Exchange Commission), 63, 64–65, 123
self-assessment, 31, 46, 52; and board of directors, 90, 93, 107, 110; TRACOM Social Style, 76, 85
Seremet, Mark E., 60, 61
shareholders, 5, 12, 38; activism of, 10, 65–66, 125, 127; commitment to, 63, 67, 116, 117, 124; and confidence, 2, 122. *See also* stakeholders
Silverthorne, Sean, 59
situation analysis, 71–72
Six Sigma quality, 37, 39–40
social capital, 111
Social Contract, 1–13; and behavioral standards, 5–11; need for, 60, 88; and partnership, 5–7, 9–10, 94, 121; process of, 11–13; at TTWO, 63, 66–67; and Tyco, 1–4
The Social Contract (Rousseau), 1
social intelligence (SI), 31, 106, 110
social styles, 17, 74, 86, 107, 111; amiable, 37–39; analytical, 31–34, 39–41; definitions of, 30–31, 32–33; driver, 34–35; expressive, 36–37; and ILM, 41–44. *See also* leadership styles
Southwest Airlines, 25, 28